America's Backpack Nuke

A True Account

Love, War, History and Drama

The Mission Was Far Beyond the Call!

D1738573

Michael P. Chapanar,
11th Engineer Battalion, 3rd Marine Division
U.S.M.C. 1967 Vietnam D.M.Z.

PAGE PUBLISHING, INC.
Conneaut Lake, PA

First originally published by Page Publishing 2020

ISBN 978-1-6624-2213-3 (pbk)
ISBN 978-1-6624-4078-6 (hc)
ISBN 978-1-6624-2214-0 (digital)

The views expressed in this publication are those of the author and do not necessarily reflect the official policy or position of the Department of Defense or the U.S. Government.

Printed in the United States of America

How many human beings on the planet
were ordered to conduct a mission
to strap on a tactical nuclear weapon
and carry it into battle to save six
thousand United States Marines?

CONTENTS

PHOTO INDEX

PROLOGUE

Living forty-five years with a classified and dynamic missing piece of Vietnam history, I struggled with issues morally and legally, finding a way to let the world know about top secret activity in Vietnam.

In 2012 I was informed, some of my military records were declassified. The story defines the how, why, when, and where in Vietnam I was tasked with strapping on a tactical nuclear weapon known today as a backpack nuke.

Although the book is about combat and nuclear weapons, it is also a human-interest and love story. Growing up I did not realize playing the game of baseball was prepping me to be a United States Marine. I had no vision of having the opportunity to work hand and hand with the CIA. Blessed with two special talents and a lot of luck, I survived the most daring work on earth. The job was so extremely dangerous, both MOS 1372 replacement Marines were separately and tragically killed pursuing the same occupational endeavors.

Prior to joining the Marine Corps at age eighteen, I was a homeless refuse worker. After joining the Marines and volunteering for Vietnam, I found myself at North Island Nuclear Weapons Training Center, U.S. Naval Air Station in San Diego, training to deploy a nuclear bomb on the battlefield. The other ingredient required was actual combat experience. While in Vietnam, the USMC ordered me away from combat on three separate occasions. I was sent each time to Okinawa to progressively learn techniques of annihilating the enemy and changing the landscape forever.

In late fall of 1967, I was given the order to strap on the bomb in Vietnam. At that point it was an all-volunteer mission and, in all probability, one I would not survive. Saving six thousand Marines was larger than one person; I had no choice.

How close we were to nuclear war on an autumn night in '67 was terrifying. The nuclear weapon training and combat experiences in the United States Marine Corps is a story within itself, but *the mission was far beyond the call.*

The world understands, a nuclear bomb did not go off in Vietnam, and for this reason, I'm alive to tell my chilling experiences.

While on a trip to Carmel-by-the-Sea in Monterey, California, Angela and I met Paul Carota and Harry O'Donnell, friends of Mr. Clint Eastwood, and they convinced me the story must be told. In 2017 we were enjoying our vacation, staying at Clint Eastwood's Mission Ranch, when we were introduced to Jamie Bosworth Sr. Jamie is an entertainer, attorney, and also a friend of the legendary actor. Without his enthusiasm, I most likely would not have continued to reveal the story. Jamie is a United States Army veteran and was convincing.

Prior to writing the book, I wanted to be confident and sure I would not be doing something detrimental or harmful to America. Although some of my records were now declassified, I didn't feel it was enough. I felt an obligation to obtain permission from the highest levels of our country in order to unveil this U.S. nuclear weapon secret undertaking.

On March 7, 2018, I mailed letters to President Trump, Secretary of Defense General James "'Mad Dog'" Mattis, and the commandant of the Marine Corps General Robert Neller. Upon receiving permission, I submitted the book/manuscript to the United States Pentagon, Department of Defense, Office of Prepublication and Security Review. It was cleared for open publication on 9/11 (September 11, 2018.)

I was still concerned and pondered for an additional two years before publishing the book. Today I'm convinced more than ever, the history needs to surface in hopes it might help avoid catastrophe in the future.

I wish to dedicate the book to all my comrades who fought for democracy in Vietnam, and God bless the souls that didn't make it out alive.

PREFACE

How many human beings on the planet train for the opportunity to strap on an atomic bomb and take it into battle to save six thousand young people you don't know, called United States Marines?

America's Backpack Nuke

The Mission Was Far Beyond the Call!

A True Story

The Question It Poses

When ego and deceit replace logic and truth in war, who on earth is *beyond the call* of destruction?

Michael P. Chapanar
Eleventh Engineer Battalion
MOS 1372 Atomic Demolition
Third Marine Division
USMC 1966/1967, Vietnam

People's Republic of China

MAP A

Buffer Zone

• Dien Bien Phu

• HANOI

NORTH VIETNAM

GULF OF TONKIN

LAOS

HAINAN ISLAND

1,575 miles to Okinawa

THAILAND

DMZ 17th PARALLEL

Khe Sanh Combat Base

LAOS

SOUTH VIETNAM

CAMBODIA

SOUTH CHINA SEA

SAIGON •

N
W E
S

VIETNAM WAR THEATER
1967-68

Prepared by
Michael Chapanar

MAP B

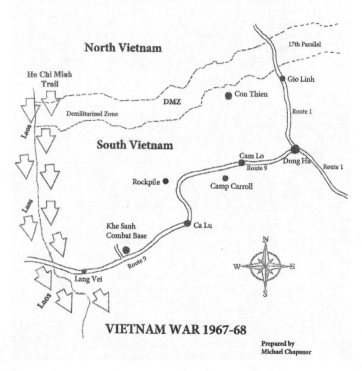

North Vietnam

17th Parallel

Ho Chi Minh Trail

Gio Linh

DMZ

Con Thien

Demilitarized Zone

Route 1

Laos

South Vietnam

Cam Lo

Dong Ha

Route 9

Route 1

Rockpile

Camp Carroll

Laos

Khe Sanh Combat Base

Ca Lu

N

Route 9

W   E

Lang Vei

S

Laos

VIETNAM WAR 1967-68

Prepared by
Michael Chapanar

People's Republic of China

MAP C

Buffer Zone

Dien Bien Phu

HANOI

NORTH VIETNAM

GULF OF TONKIN

LAOS

HAINAN ISLAND

1,575 miles to Okinawa

DMZ 17th PARALLEL

Khe Sanh Combat Base

THAILAND

LAOS

Da Nang

I Corps

Kon Tum

John Paul Vann's Helicopter Crash

SOUTH VIETNAM

II Corps

CAMBODIA

SOUTH CHINA SEA

SAIGON

III Corps

IV Corps

N
W E
S

VIETNAM WAR THEATER
1967-68

Prepared by
Michael Chapanar

CHAPTER 1

Protection from Humiliation

America simply refers to the war as the Vietnam War. The Vietnamese people labeled the war the Resistance War Against America. The Vietnam Cold War started in 1955, and the United States buildup was escalated under President John F. Kennedy. The U.S. Government sent more than sixteen thousand military advisers to South Vietnam during the period from 1959 through 1963 to train and advise the South Vietnamese military. Soon after Kennedy's assassination in 1963 President Lyndon B. Johnson increased the number of military advisers to twenty-three thousand. The Johnson administration increased U.S. military presence in Vietnam every year of his presidency.

I was in the Marine Corps from January 1966 through January 1972. By the time I arrived in Vietnam, November '66, we already had three hundred eighty-five thousand men in the country with an additional sixty thousand sailors stationed offshore. During my time in Vietnam our U.S. troop level rose to more than four hundred-eighty thousand in the country.

During my first year in the Marines, I embraced serious and comprehensive training, using big-league explosives. When I finally arrived in Vietnam at the ripe old age of nineteen, my innocence was gone.

The area around the demilitarized zone (DMZ) was my home in the months to follow, and I had no chance of extricating myself from this debacle.

America paid a terrible price in its Vietnam War, trying to halt the spread of communism with nearly sixty thousand U.S. soldiers killed in action, over one hundred fifty thousand wounded, and more than one thousand six hundred missing. The ground war in South Vietnam also included sections of Laos and Cambodia bordering Vietnam to the west. Estimates of Vietnamese soldiers and civilians killed varied widely. Up to three and one-half million Vietnamese people died in the war. Some two hundred-seventy thousand or more Cambodians perished, and more than twenty-eight thousand Laotian people were said to have lost their lives in the conflict.

The Ho Chi Minh trail traversed north to south through the mountains and valleys of Western Vietnam while extending into Eastern Laos and Cambodia as well. The Ho Chi Minh trail was used extensively throughout the war by the Communist North Vietnamese to resupply troops and arms into the south. It was North Vietnam's main infiltration route (refer to map B, p. 24). During the fall of 1967 the Communist forces were pouring down the trail into South Vietnam along the Laotian border and around the DMZ. It had been the job of the United States Marine Corps to halt the infiltration and hold the DMZ intact. Keeping our own U.S. Marine supply lines open to our forward firebases presented unimaginable challenges. Without the American bases at Khe Sanh and Con Thien on the DMZ, the Communist aggression into South Vietnam would have happened unimpeded at a much quicker pace. Some of the fiercest fighting of the war took place in I-Corps on the DMZ. Perhaps, in the end, our only accomplishment was that we helped slow down the inevitable.

During my time in Nam, Ho Chi Minh (Ho-chee-min) served as president of North Vietnam. He served as president from 1945 to 1969. He was often referred to as Uncle Ho by his people. Uncle Ho was known to have lived under more than fifty different names. It is generally accepted that he was born in 1890, and for a time, he lived in France, the United States, the United Kingdom, Russia, and China. In 1941 he went home to Vietnam and formed a revolutionary group for the independence movement of Vietnam. He called his Communist revolutionaries the Viet Minh. His main goal in life from 1941 until the end of his life was to see his country of Vietnam free themselves from foreign occupation and domination. In earlier years it was the French occupation, and then it was the Japanese occupation during World War II. After World War II it went back to French occupation, and a war between the French and Vietnamese people was on the horizon.

In 1946 Ho Chi Minh did declare war against the French, marking the beginning of the First Indochina War. Minh's North Vietnamese National Army attacked the French occupation of Vietnam, and the war was on.

In 1950, four years after the start of the war, Ho Chi Minh met with the Soviet Union and Chinese leaders. The leaders agreed, from that point on, Communist China would back the Viet Minh. The Viet Minh's forces would receive from China additional supplies, training, and arms, allowing them to ramp up the war against the French regime throughout the region. Ho's main thought in the war was, "You can kill ten of my men for every one I kill of yours, but in the end you will lose, and I will win." The war lasted four more years, and Ho Chi Minh was proven right.

The First Indochina War ended in 1954 with a stunning Communist victory at Dien Bien Phu. North Vietnamese Communist forces (Viet Minh) secretly maneuvered roughly fifty thousand troops into the hills surrounding a French-held valley. On their way to the battlefield, men, women, and children were pulling, pushing, and dragging vast amounts of heavy artillery, mortars, ammunition, food, and equipment with them. A very important French combat base was located at the bottom of the basin and was the direct target of the Viet Minh. The French had an estimated fifteen thousand men readily available to defend their monsoon-affected combat base. French commanders were very much overconfident and were under the impression they were the ones who had the superior firepower. The French were eager to have a decisive battle with the Viet Minh. They also thought they would finally have a great opportunity to lure the Viet Minh out into the open and away from the hills and tunnels, only to destroy them. Just one problem—the French, with all their fortifications, aviation, paratroopers, and massive firepower, were wrong. They would soon discover they were outplanned, outmanned, and outgunned. Their idea to destroy the Viet Minh at Dien Bien Phu was a catastrophic blunder. The French were completely duped and were totally unaware of the planning that was orchestrated and put in place the preceding days, weeks, and months to savagely overrun the entire French-held valley. The Viet Minh's plan to encircle and destroy the base with ferocious and overwhelming artillery attacks pulverizing the base began on March 13. Meanwhile, staggering waves of ground forces inched down from the hills closer and closer to kill or capture whatever survived their well-planned, agonizing artillery barrage. At one point during the fifty-seven-day siege, the French were offered and considered the use of nuclear weapons to stave off the ongoing brutal attack that was shredding the base to pieces.

American Diplomat John Foster Dulles reportedly mentioned the unthinkable idea of the United States lending atomic bombs to the French for use at Dien Bien Phu.

Needless to say, no atomic bombs were ever lent by the United States. In the end the Viet Minh captured several thousand battered French soldiers, of which about half died in captivity. Few more than one thousand escaped the valley while their remaining troops were slaughtered. The siege put an end to French occupation and the First Indochina War in Vietnam. Shortly after conclusion of the war, the country of Vietnam was divided into two halves. The Communist-held northern half was divided from the non-communist southern half at the seventeenth parallel, later known as the demilitarized zone (DMZ) (refer to map C, p. 25).

Thirteen years later, in the fall of '67, there were similar happenings unfolding in and around the DMZ. The U.S. combat base known as Khe Sanh was located sixteen miles south of the DMZ and seven miles east of the Laotian border. The monsoon-affected base was becoming a real concern for President Lyndon B. Johnson (LBJ), Secretary of Defense, Robert S. McNamara, and General William Westmoreland (Westy), commander of all U.S. forces in Vietnam.

The U.S. Senate minority leader of the Democratic Party in 1954 was Lyndon Baines Johnson. It was LBJ who had a bird's-eye view, listening to reports and watching on TV General Giap destroy the French at the infamous Battle of Dien Bien Phu. In 1954 Johnson came to realize what Giap was capable of, and it never left his memory. Thirteen years later when he himself was now facing Giap head-on, the total recall of that battle was foremost in the center of his mind.

President Johnson told McNamara and Westmoreland that he did not want a repeat of Dien Bien Phu at Khe Sanh or anywhere else. The battle brewing at Khe Sanh was now starting to look like what took place back in 1954. I believe Westmoreland was worried that if we lost the combat base at Khe Sanh, the United States would go on to lose the entire war just as France had lost their war to the same strong-willed Vietnamese people. As the weeks progressed, the situation building around Khe Sanh was seemingly exactly the same as what took place earlier at Dien Bien Phu. The rainy season and the buildup of North Vietnamese troops in the fall of '67 presented the reality of Communist forces overrunning our irreplaceable, strategic firebase, and the likelihood was quickly becoming a grave threat.

Khe Sanh had fewer than six thousand military ground personnel, mostly U.S. Marines defending it at the time. LBJ, McNamara, and Westy had drawn the conclusion that an attempt by the North Vietnamese Army to pull off a repeat of Dien Bien Phu was in the works. Khe Sanh as well as Con Thien and other U.S. Marine combat bases on the DMZ were all within range of North Vietnamese heavy artillery and rockets from the surrounding hills and from inside North Vietnam across the DMZ. The U.S. Marines were in difficult positions and were being pounded daily.

The fall months of '67 were confusing times for President Johnson. General Westmoreland reported the United States was winning the war of attrition with an overwhelming, deadly body count of 10-1, and we had reached the crossover point. Meanwhile, the North Vietnamese Army (NVA) and Viet Cong (VC) were amassing more than forty thousand troops and personnel in and around the DMZ with up to twenty thousand more on their way, filtering down the Ho Chi Minh trail. How could Westmoreland's assessment of his war-of-attrition scenario be accurate? Should the slaughter of a U.S. firebase take place, the people back home would discover they were being badly misled, and this could end any remaining support for the war.

Using a tactical nuclear weapon to stop the enemy dead in their tracks while at the same time sending a psychological and convincing message to Hanoi was assuredly in our playbook, and no one had to lend the United States the bomb. An individual combat Marine was expendable, and I was now fully trained to carry the bomb to the battlefield. I was dead certain I would be given the order to light up the weapon. Any information to the contrary was absent. The USMC made it clear to me, there might be no other way to save our Marines from being slaughtered. During the monsoon season when our air support was limited or completely nonexistent would be the ideal time for the Communist to destroy the base with artillery and then completely overrun the base with their ground forces.

I was convinced my days on earth were drawing down. I truly understood the purpose of my being. I remember going over in my mind how all this came to pass. Just a couple dozen months ago I met a girl and fell deeply in love. I was also playing a game I loved (baseball). Now, I was trained to kill and mentally capable of vaporizing masses of human beings in the tens of thousands that included myself. Claustrophobia was my one Achilles' heel I had to overcome and deal with on a daily basis. I couldn't tell anyone about my claustrophobic mental feelings, and I had no way out of doing my job. I thought of how I would be remembered. Would I go down in history as good or evil? Would I go to heaven or hell?

Shortly after my last of three top secret nuclear weapon training trips to Okinawa, the USMC and CIA said they needed to know my whereabouts 24-7.

After extensive combat participation in and around the DMZ my first nine months, I was removed from all field combat operations. I was ordered back inside the gates of the Dong Ha Combat Base in September of 1967. Our battalion commander had a small barbershop constructed less than twenty feet from our tent, and he told me I was now a barber. I was also instructed never to stray from the immediate area and barbershop. I needed to be there and ready to deploy. I was permitted to go to the mess hall about one hundred twenty yards away, no farther. Then from out of nowhere, rehearsal deployment drills with a tactical backpack nuclear weapon would constantly occur when I least expected. The USMC was continuously evaluating my reliability, preparation, willingness, and ability to do the mission weekly and sometimes daily. Up till now history has never examined or exposed the preparation and planning to use a tactical nuclear weapon *in the fall of 1967*. At that particular time the use of a tactical nuclear bomb was, perhaps, never more important in the war. The area around the DMZ was sparsely populated, and this could limit collateral damage. With winds blowing out of the south to the north, no U.S. troops would be in harm's way of radiation, and it was planned, no U.S. personnel would be north of the blast zone. The geographical layouts and the timing of massive enemy troops gathering in one or two general regions around the DMZ presented prime opportunities. Other crucial elements needed were meteorological, precise timing and a way to strike the target with precision. With inconsistent weather the exact day or week to strike by air could change rapidly. Hitting a moving target under these conditions would be a real stretch. A ground-pounding Marine setting off a nuclear bomb precisely where and when needed was the strategy. A U.S. Marine deploying the bomb and staying close to the weapon until detonation also offered the option to call off the mission up to the very last second. The USMC finally had the right time, the right place, and the right Marine to accomplish the mission while sending a message to Hanoi and, perhaps, ending the war.

The North Vietnamese commanding general, General Vo Nguyen Giap, was thought to be one of the greatest military strategists of the past century. He first rose to height in World War II when he served as leader of the Viet Minh resistance against the Japanese in Vietnam. General Giap was a momentous military commander in two wars—the First Indochina War and the Vietnam War. He played a big part in some of the world's most historical battles during his time. The Battle of Dien Bien Phu in 1954 was his most glorious victory. Giap was a strategic mastermind of artillery. He was also instrumental in laying the foundation of the Ho Chi Minh trail, which is, perhaps, one of the greatest masterstrokes of military engineering in the last one hundred years. He was brilliant at logistics, showing his prominence in the hills surrounding Dien Bien Phu and again in the planning and carrying out the siege of Khe Sanh as well as launching the Tet Offensive. Ho Chi Minh, the president of Vietnam, had a loyal and masterful tactician in General Giap. As a mastermind who always left his ego behind, Giap had his troops in both 1954 and again in 1967–68 on their hands and knees, pushing and dragging massive amounts of artillery up and over mountains and through tunnels. His troops crossed many streams and rivers, wading through jungle and rice paddies along the way. Most of this work was done at night while overcoming inclement weather, wild animals, snakes, bombings, illnesses, and injuries. He then successfully encouraged his armies of men and women to fight to the death at their final destinations. The logistics of such unimaginable operations would go largely unnoticed by his adversaries. Giap was a genius.

In 1967 the combat base at Khe Sanh and the surrounding hills in the DMZ area were looking to be a repeat performance of his victory against the French at Dien Bien Phu. The grim similarities were unmistakable, and the

United States was determined not to let this happen. The Khe Sanh Combat Base (KSCB) situation did not go unnoticed by Johnson, McNamara, or General Westmoreland. Although the U.S. high command first thought combat operations being carried out by the North Vietnamese Army around Khe Sanh were likely a series of minor offensives, their thoughts were clearly changing.

The United States responded with a buildup of the isolated Marine base to approximately six thousand military personnel. During this time, all U.S. outposts on hilltops surrounding the base were subject to constant artillery, mortar, and rocket fire. U.S. Air Force, Navy, and Marine aircraft stepped up massive aerial bombardments, dropping tens of thousands of bombs in support of the Marines. On January 21, 1968, vast amounts of NVA enemy artillery ferociously began falling on the base. Nine days later, on

January 30, the Tet Offensive attacks were set in motion to overrun the entire country of South Vietnam and not just Khe Sanh.

A few months earlier, during the unpredictable fog and rainy season in the fall of '67, General Westmoreland had a mindset of using a tactical nuclear weapon. At that time, he wanted to use the bomb as a *proactive* measure to prevent annihilation of the Marines at Khe Sanh. The *New York Times* printed a story in October 2018 about recent uncovered top secret documents that showed undeniable evidence that in 1968 Westmoreland was serious about the use of nuclear weapons. The front-page story revealed that in the early months of '68 Westmoreland had an idea of using one or more nuclear weapons as a *reactive* counterattack measure to save the base and, perhaps, the entire war. Johnson and Westmoreland were working closely together, and both men realized what a fearful and overwhelming opponent the United States was facing when the president insisted the base was to be saved at all cost. A humiliating and embarrassing defeat at Khe Sanh was not an option. Neither Johnson nor Westmoreland had any ambition to be the first American commanders to lose a foreign war. Both men had to protect themselves from political disaster with a war that could end in humiliation. I could conjure up no idea of making it out of this conundrum alive.

CHAPTER 2

The Soldier of Vietnam

John Vann, perhaps, had more influence in the war than our family originally thought. John Paul Vann was my second cousin through marriage to Mary Jane Allen.

Vann first started his Vietnam crusade at age thirty-seven. He completed twenty years of service to his country and retired from the U.S. Army as a lieutenant colonel on July 31, 1963.

His first tour in Vietnam began in March of 1962, and he dedicated the next ten years of his life to the war. As a civilian, he went back to Vietnam in 1965 in the position of provincial pacification representative with the

U.S. Agency for International Development (AID). In 1967 Vann put himself in a position of disfavor with General Westmoreland and much of the hierarchy in authority. Westmoreland made an assessment, the war of attrition was working.

Meanwhile, Vann came to the conclusion, the Vietnamese Communists were stronger than ever, and the war of attrition was *not* working. John Vann was vindicated on January 31, 1968, when Communist-led forces took advantage of the Vietnamese Lunar New Year. The NVA and VC Communist forces commenced attacks on most cities, towns, and installations in South Vietnam. It was called the Tet Offensive.

The war-of-attrition strategy General Westmoreland pursued was totally discredited, and Westmoreland was relieved as commanding general in Vietnam.

John's closest friend, Daniel Ellsberg, who earlier had been a comrade with him in Vietnam for more than nineteen months, had returned home to America in June of 1967. Ellsberg concluded, the violence in Vietnam was so senseless and immoral that his own conscience said he had to put forth an effort to end the war.

Ellsberg was now trying to stop the war with his antiwar crusade while Vann continued his crusade to *win the war* his own way. Although each took separate paths, their friendship remained strong. In 1972 Daniel Ellsberg was preparing to go on trial in the federal district court in Los Angeles for copying what was known as the *Pentagon Papers*. John Vann told Ellsberg he would testify in his favor. Vann had risen in the system although he was thought of as a maverick. His disagreements over strategies and tactics were always in light of winning the war in the most efficient way. Vann had leadership qualities and dedication that did not go unnoticed by those in authority in Washington and Saigon. In 1971 John Vann was assigned to a position as senior adviser to the core region of the Central Highlands along with adjacent provinces on the Central Coastline. He was put in charge of all U.S. military forces in this area, including the civilians and military officers assigned to the pacification program. He also covertly shared command of one hundred fifty-eight thousand South Vietnamese troops. This appointment was unprecedented in the American history of wars, being that John Vann was technically a civilian employed by AID. The position, in effect, was equivalent to a major general in the U.S. Army. His accumulated expertise, leadership qualities, and willingness to take a calculated risk made him one of the most irreplaceable Americans.

John's best friend, Daniel Ellsberg, was also very instrumental in the war.

The following are excerpts from Daniel Ellsberg's bio, maintained by his son Michael Ellsberg.

> In 1959, Daniel Ellsberg became a strategic analyst at the RAND Corporation, and consultant to the Defense Department and the White House specializing in problems of the command and control of nuclear weapons, nuclear war plans and crisis decision-making. In 1961 he drafted the guidance from Secretary of Defense Robert McNamara to the Joint Chiefs of Staff on the operational plans for general nuclear war. He was

a member of two of the three working groups reporting to the Executive Committee of the National Security Council (EXCOM) during the Cuban Missile Crisis in 1962.

Ellsberg joined the Defense Department in 1964 as Special Assistant to Assistant Secretary of Defense (International Security Affairs) John McNaughton, working on the escalation of the war in Vietnam. He transferred to the State Department in 1965 to serve two years at the U.S. Embassy in Saigon, Vietnam evaluating pacification in the field.

On return to the RAND Corporation in 1967, Ellsberg worked on the top secret McNamara study of *U.S. Decision-making in Vietnam*, 1945-68, which later came to be known as the Pentagon Papers. In 1969, he secretly photocopied the 7,000 page study and gave it to the Senate Foreign Relations Committee; in 1971 he gave it to the *New York Times,* the *Washington Post* and 17 other newspapers. His trial, on twelve felony counts posing a possible sentence of 115 years, was dismissed in 1973 on grounds of governmental misconduct against him, which led to the convictions of several White House aides and figured in the impeachment proceedings against President Nixon.

Daniel Ellsberg is the author of the following books: *The Doomsday Machine: Confessions of a Nuclear War Planner* (2017); *Secrets: A Memoir of Vietnam and the Pentagon Papers* (2002); *Risk, Ambiguity and Decision* (2001); and *Papers on the War* (1971). Since the end of the Vietnam War, Ellsberg has been a lecturer, writer and activist on the dangers of the nuclear war era, wrongful U.S. interventions and the urgent need for patriotic whistleblowing.[1]

---

[1] Michael Ellsberg, "Daniel Ellsberg: Bio," https://www.ellsberg.net/bio/.

CHAPTER 3

Family

My mother, Jeanne Andrews-Chapanar, is the daughter of Nick Andrews. Nick had two siblings—a brother, George, and a sister, Mary. Nick's sister married Jess Allen.

Aunt Mary and Uncle Jess were parents of Doris and Mary Jane Allen. Mary Jane wed her high-school sweetheart, John Paul Vann, on October 6, 1945.

Aunt Mary and Uncle Jess lived in New York. Several times a year, Mother would drive my grandfather Nick, Uncle George, and me from our home in Canton, Ohio, to Rochester, New York. Aunt Mary would always invite us to stay overnight. She would also invite her daughter, Mary Jane, over to the house when we came up. Mary Jane and Mother were not only cousins, but they also grew up together as best friends. It was a reunion of sorts. John Vann was an officer in the Army at the time, and Mother would coordinate the trips with Mary Jane when she knew John would be home. Mary Jane and John enjoyed these special times. At our evening dinners, John was very quiet at the table and would only speak when spoken to. The usual protocol after dinner was, the women would head for the kitchen to clean up, and the men would head for the living room around the fireplace or to the front porch.

Uncle George was a decorated World War I combat veteran. He enlisted in the U.S. Army on June 24, 1916. He was a corporal in the Army and served in France. George received a wonderful decoration, the "*Le President des A.C. de Verdun*" Medal. George was my favorite uncle and, although small in stature, was a giant of a man at only five-foot-four-inches tall. George was fifty-one years older than me, but we were as close as brothers. It was George who actually raised my mother, Jeanne, in the hardest of times. George was proud of his nephew, and we had a special relationship. It was special because George was special.

Around the fireplace or on the front porch after dinner, George would tell us stories about his combat escapades in World War I. John was fascinated and asked endless questions about George's combat. Vann was born and raised in Norfolk, Virginia; therefore, he was interested in George's stories about running whiskey and booze from the West Virginia border up through Ohio and into Detroit. In the roaring twenties, George had a hot-rod car. It had two tanks converted into one—one side of the tank for gasoline and the other for booze. Running booze was the way George made a living back then. He had a route. When police would give him a chase, he would quickly outrun the cops with his souped-up car.

George was as proud as a peacock and would tell John about every little detail. Aunt Mary and Uncle Jess had a vineyard in the backyard of their beautiful home, and after storytelling, we would end up in the backyard, picking Concord grapes. I would take my glove, some balls, and a bat to Rochester on every trip. John enjoyed hitting ground balls to me for hours, and we had a lot of fun. If it was cold or raining, we would finish off the night with some competitive ping-pong matches in the basement recreation room. Although John was very quiet at the dinner table, he had a sense of humor. On one occasion, he handed me a basket for picking grapes. I went to the backyard in hopes of finding an abundance of ripe grapes, but could not find a single one. Upon return, John told me to sit down and relax. He would find some. One minute later he returned with a full basket of plump, ripe grapes. The girls had now joined us on the front porch when my aunt Mary asked John if those were the grapes he spent an hour picking earlier in the day. John looked at me cross-eyed, trying not to laugh when he answered, "Yep." John always enjoyed joking around, making us laugh.

(Top) Mary Jane Vann, John Paul Vann with son, John Allen Vann, and daughter, Patricia, at Aunt Mary and Uncle Jess's home in New York.

(Bottom) Michael's little brother, Tim, on the left and Michael on the right in front of the fireplace while visiting Aunt Mary. Mary Jane's beautiful wedding picture sitting on the mantel.

(Pictures courtesy of Michael Chapanar.)

Michael's mother, Michael, and Uncle George.
(Picture courtesy of Michael Chapanar.)

I remember one year playing Little League Baseball. John and Mary Jane Vann were in town, visiting my mother. I was so excited when the whole family decided to come watch me play a game. John sat in the dugout with our team. Aunt Mary and Uncle Jess were also in Canton and attended the game. On one occasion Angela and I were out of town when Aunt Mary with her daughters, Doris and Mary Jane, came into town. Mother had them stay at our home while we were on vacation. George was always tickled when the family came to visit. Aunt Mary was a sweetheart.

Mom, Aunt Mary, and Angela with Uncle George in the background.

(Picture courtesy of Michael Chapanar.)

CHAPTER 4

Childhood

Childhood was extremely influential on the decision I made to join the Marine Corps and volunteer for Vietnam.

When I was a little boy, we would play cowboys and Indians. Pretending to be the Lone Ranger with a white hat and mask was fun. I watched *The Lone Ranger* on TV every afternoon. The Lone Ranger and Tonto were always saving the day and riding off into the sunset, yelling, "Hi ho silver!" They were to be admired. The Lone Ranger and Tonto always made good decisions.

The cartoon called *Popeye the Sailor* followed *The Lone Ranger*. Popeye's crusade was forever fighting to win his girlfriend Olive Oyl's love. Bluto, the sailor, was the adversarial villain while Popeye was the good guy. Popeye would justly win and save the day. Popeye knew, Olive Oyl's love was the ultimate prize. Olive had big, dark eyes, long hair, and a very skinny, stick-figured body.

One common characteristic both Popeye and the Lone Ranger had in common was, they would never give up and always triumph in their quest.

A few years later, the neighborhood kids moved on from playing cowboys and Indians. It was a time to play Army, hide out, make tunnels, and play war games. We had wooden guns and light bags of dust we threw at one another, pretending they were hand grenades. We were great at making machine-gun noises. When playing Army, I always pretended to be John Paul Vann. Likewise, when playing whiffle ball, I pretended to be a New York

Yankee baseball star. I did a lot of pretending back then. Soon I was a U.S. Marine trained to carry a backpack nuclear weapon on the Vietnam DMZ, and I was not pretending anymore.

The journey

One day the school announced it was having tryouts for a Little League team. I was eight years old when I signed up. Two of the coaches asked if I thought I was big enough to play Little League Baseball, and I said, "Yep." The school was five miles away from our home, and we had bus transportation to and from school. Along the way, there were steep hills, and some were over three hundred feet high. Our Little League team practiced three times a week in the evening, and there was no bus transportation.

Mom and Dad were both working. Mother was working part-time, and we only had one car. I rode a rickety old bike to the baseball field behind the school. At first I could only reach the top of each hill after several stops to rest. As time progressed, I could make it up all the hills without stopping.

I loved baseball and was a New York Yankee fan. Canton, Ohio, was sixty miles south of Cleveland, and it was a big deal when the Yankees played the Indians. I didn't know at the time, I would go on to play seven years of amateur baseball with and against a future New York Yankee World Series champion star catcher and captain, Thurman Munson. We were both the same age. After many years of thinking Thurm was so lucky to go on and play for the New York Yankees, he was suddenly killed. Sadly, I was one of the first to arrive on scene at the plane-crash site that killed Thurm on that fateful afternoon of August 2, 1979. I knew all three passengers aboard; Jerry and David survived. Thurman did not. It was heart-wrenching.

Michael is standing next to the emergency vehicle at the plane crash.

Picture courtesy of WPIX affiliate FOX 8 News–Cleveland Ohio.

Our first Little League season finally got underway, and we were playing two games along with three practices a week. I was riding my bike ten miles round trip to the baseball field five times a week (fifty miles total.) Not yet big enough or good enough to play first string, I was given the chore of catching batting practice while the other fourteen kids batted for two hours. I was constantly bending down and getting back up with every pitch. Being the practice catcher wore my legs out; then I had to ride my bike five miles home. I had no idea my legs were going to become so strong. I just loved to play baseball. I also liked catching although I was so small, a part of the chest protector hung down and was dragging on the ground even after I stood up. More so, when I bent down to catch a ball, it was dragging on the ground. Coach John noticed the dragging, and I was tagged with the name Peter Dragon. I was always tripping on it, so Coach John cut that piece off. The chest protector was tailor-made by cutting off the piece that protected your privates. I was so tiny that without this part of the chest protector, it would still protect that very important area.

The following year, I made the varsity team, and for the next three years, I rode my bike back and forth. I was the littlest guy on the team, and although not very fast, I had endurance and a lot of talent for the game. Now playing first string and still catching batting practices, I could hop up like a frog and throw out anyone trying to steal second base. The legs continued getting stronger.

We were all good Little League players, and we won the championship for the school's first ever Little League title, and I was named the most valuable player.

Little League team picture.

Michael kneeling, bottom row,
second from right.

(Picture courtesy of Michael Chapanar.)

From age thirteen to sixteen, we all played on several different baseball teams each year. We had neighborhood teams, traveling teams, and all-star teams. I thought, for sure, this was the road to the New York Yankees, and I loved playing baseball from morning to night. Because of growth spurts, I contracted a disease called Osgood-Schlatter's. This disease involved the shinbone (tibia) below the kneecap. The tendon (patellar tendon) tore away from the shinbone and became inflamed; the pain was unbearable. Both legs had to be put in casts for eight weeks—first, one leg and then the other. However, with this treatment, once the knees were healed, the disease would never return.

I acquired the disease during my sophomore year, wrestling for Perry High School. If I captured someone in my scissors leg hold, I'd squeeze the breath out of them. It was a great move, and very few could escape.

I believe, the pressure I was putting on my knees, using this hold, was one of the reasons they tore apart.

As a sophomore I stood five feet tall and weighed a whopping one hundred eighteen pounds.

I was always looking up at the pretty girls. The following year I became a freak of nature and grew six inches, putting on twenty-seven pounds. The next year I grew another six inches and put on another twenty pounds. At six feet, one hundred sixty-five pounds, most girls were looking up and barely recognized me.

As a junior on the varsity baseball team for Perry High School, I was again bending up and down as a catcher, and I still liked catching batting practice. The team liked it too; nobody else had to get behind the plate, and the legs were getting stronger.

In my junior year, Mom and Dad divorced and went their separate ways. Mother left Ohio and went to Kentucky with my two younger brothers and her new husband while I stayed behind.

Dad was not fond of any of his three sons and was unhappy with the way the marriage ended. He was disgruntled and bitter. Dad didn't want anything to do with his sons; therefore, I didn't have a place to live. Basically, I was homeless with an old, beat-up car. One day I crossed over a bumpy railroad track, and the car locked up. The rear wheels wouldn't turn anymore as if the emergency brake was on, and that was the end of the car. The junkyard paid me twenty dollars for the car. Prior to the railroad-track incident, the car was my home. I slept in the Perry parking lot for several months, and each morning I would get up and go to a friend's home to shower and clean up. I had only two sets of clothes left to wear after my freak of growth spurts. I never wanted to sleep overnight at anyone's home or make a nuisance of myself, so I lived and slept in the Perry parking lot. It was something I needed to do in order to play baseball with my friends and graduate from Perry. I also didn't have much money for gas, but I did have a magic rubber hose. I'd park that old car next to another car and siphon out his gas into my tank. In less than five minutes I magically had a tank of gas. I had no money to even buy a much-desired junior or senior high-school annual. I didn't have any money—period. Raking up apples for twenty cents an hour was hardly enough to buy food. One day I was offered a job to work for a friend's father who owned a refuse company. The job was carrying garbage. I started picking up garbage after school and throughout the summer during the day. In the summer I played baseball at night and also on days I was not hauling garbage. I was a garbage man picking up garbage for a small hourly rate. Back then they had galvanized cans that could be very heavy. I walked from the truck to the customer's backyard where everyone kept their garbage can as far away from the house as possible. The cans would smell badly, and at times they were full of maggots. People would throw everything in their can—old bricks, pieces of cement, and anything else they wanted to get rid of. The cans would sometimes rust out and break up while I was carrying them. The maggots would fall into your hair and down inside your clothing—not fun! You would continuously bring each can from a customer's backyard to the street, dump it into the truck, and return the empty can. It was a garbage route, and almost everyone used the same garbage company. It was nonstop bending down and standing back up with a garbage can over your head and on your shoulder. Sometimes these garbage cans weighed up to seventy-five pounds or more. You were essentially doing squats all day. Being a baseball catcher and now a garbageman was making for some powerful legs. I began taking up martial arts in my junior year at the YMCA. I was very quick and excellent at kicking. I never played high-school football although I had some fun on the football field, kicking field goals. I was able to kick forty-five-yard field goals with ease, but baseball was my game, and I didn't want to hurt my knees again by playing football.

When wrestling, if I put someone in the scissors-and-leg hold, they could not escape. The hand-eye coordination from baseball and karate helped with overall fighting skills.

Michael Chapanar at age seventeen.

(Picture courtesy of Michael Chapanar.)

CHAPTER 5

Angela

I met the love of my life during my senior year of high school while attending an Our Lady of Peace (OLOP) church dance across town. A church dance was held in their basement every couple of weeks for teens. One Friday night, my buddy Mickey and I heard about these dances and decided to go. We started circling around the dance floor, and I spotted the prettiest girl I had ever put eyes on. I told my friend I was going to marry that girl. He thought I was nuts, talking about marriage. Mick said, "At some point you should stop and talk to the girl first." We circled around, and I told him, "I'm going to stop and talk to her this time. She's not dancing, and I'm not going to miss the chance." I walked up to her and said, "Hi, my name is Michael, what's your name?" She replied, "Angela Russo, R-u-s-s-o." She said it so fast and spelled her last name, Russo. I said, "Who?" Again she said, "Angela R-u-s-s-o," spelling out her last name. She was nervous and, years later, admitted it was the only time she ever spelled out her last name for a boy. After a couple of dances, I asked her if she had a way home. She told me she did, and it would be impossible to go home with me tonight. She said, "You see that guy at the door with a gun on his side? That's the sheriff, and he's my father." I asked for her phone number instead. I was a senior in high school when I met her, and the following week I turned eighteen. My birthday was on April 26. I was celebrating my eighteenth birthday when I called her. I didn't tell her I was a garbageman, let alone explain how

I was homeless and living in my car. At the time, I was starting to reacquaint myself with my dad. He found out I was homeless and asked me to move in with him if I would not interfere with any of his activities. Dad was living in a small apartment and had a lot of female friends. He was age thirty-nine and in the prime of his life. Dad wanted privacy, and this arrangement didn't work out for long. He allowed me to stay with him for only a few weeks before being thrown out.

I was homeless again, and it put me back in the Perry High School parking lot. The month of April in Ohio was cold. The car at night was colder. A good friend of mine gave me several blankets, which helped.

Eventually, Mother moved back to Ohio with her new husband, and I was able to move in with her and my two brothers for the time being. This was so different, and I didn't feel right living there with her new husband; it's just the way it had to be. I was actually homeless by choice. Mother would have gladly taken me with her to Kentucky. Baseball and now Angela were reasons I stayed behind. In 1964 I was a junior in high school and had played with or against every kid on our high-school baseball team for the previous seven or eight years. It was going to be a good team, and there was little doubt we were going to win the Federal League high school baseball title. How was I going to say goodbye and move three hundred seventy-five miles south to a place I knew no one? I couldn't bring myself to leave Perry High School and life-long friends.

I made the only choice I could make. It turned out to be the best decision I ever made. We won the baseball title, and the following year I graduated from Perry. I learned the value of hard work, picking up garbage, and the value of a dollar. I found out I could make it on my own, and best of all, I met Angela.

Now eighteen years old and graduating in June, I received a birthday-and-graduation present in one envelope. It was a draft card, and I was now facing the military draft. Nobody wanted to leave home, and certainly, no one wanted to leave their girlfriend. I definitely did not want to stop playing baseball to fight a war I knew nothing about on the other side of the world. Just the same, we didn't want to be cowards or unpatriotic. I had to do the right thing; remember the Lone Ranger and Popeye? I wanted to make Angela proud and needed to do something good for the country.

Suddenly, in a blink of an eye, things were heating up in Vietnam. I was concerned as the months passed, and everyone was being drafted. Four months after I graduated from high school, I joined the Marine Corps. I took

Angela to my senior prom and was fortunate enough to have a two-week furlough the following year, allowing me to take Angela to her senior prom. I now had a wonderful girlfriend, and it didn't take long to fall in love.

Michael taking Angela to her senior prom.
(Picture courtesy of Michael Chapanar.)

CHAPTER 6

Glued In

The summer after graduating from high school, I carried garbage until I was hired by Goodyear Tire & Rubber Company in the glue division. Occasionally, at the end of a workday, being a little high from the smell of glue, I would do some funny things. It was now September of 1965, and Angela was starting her senior year of high school. She went to Glenwood, and I went to Perry, but had already graduated. Angela and I attended different high schools together. I knew her senior year was getting underway, and the first week of a new school year everything would be hectic. One day I decided to go to her school and find her. I followed her into one of her study halls, but she had not yet seen me. She sat down at a cafeteria table, talking with a friend. She looked to her left, and there I was sitting beside her. She was startled and yipped out, "What are you doing here? You shouldn't be here, you already graduated, and you didn't go to this school to begin with." I said, "They don't know that." When the teacher came around to take attendance, my name was not on the roster. I told the cafeteria study-hall teacher I was directed to come down to this study hall. It was perfect! I even gave the teacher a fake last name. The teacher said, "Okay, grab a seat." I attended her study hall every day for the next two weeks. The study-hall teacher actually thought I went to her school. They thought I was still in high school.

Meanwhile, I was getting quality time with Angela, and I knew I had to be there every day. After a couple of weeks, one day I couldn't be there. The following day the teacher asked, "Where were you yesterday? You need to go down to the office and get an excuse note because you were not here yesterday. You need a signed excuse." I knew if I went down to the office, I would be in a lot of trouble, so I left and never attended her study hall again. I did manage to sneak back into Angela's school and peek at her through the window in class a few times. Her dark eyes would get so big.

At about this time my mom was back from Kentucky with my two brothers. It was the middle of September 1965, and Mom knew a lot more about the war than I did. She thought she would try to enroll me in college at Kent State at the last minute. I knew I didn't have the grades to go to college, nor did I pay much attention in high school. I was playing a lot of baseball, carrying garbage, doing karate, and was in love. Things were bleak for college. I had no chance of succeeding in college, and it would be a waste of time. All things considered, Mom hauled me up to Kent State. They took my information, application, etc. and surprisingly, I was accepted. I was scared to death. I just didn't resemble the kids at Kent State. They had long hair and psychedelic flowery, colorful clothing, and the smell of pot was everywhere. They were all peaceniks. I had not indulged in drinking, smoking, or using drugs and thought to myself, *How in the world am I ever going to fit in with this group?*

Roger, a good friend of mine, was also set to start his freshman year at Kent, and both of us had classes starting the same day and time. Roger said we should drive up to school together. Going from Canton, Ohio, up to the city of Kent was a forty-mile trip passing through Akron, Ohio. Roger picked me up that day, and I was very apprehensive about going to college. A big problem was trying to figure out a way to pay for a college education. Upon getting close to Akron, I said to Roger, "We need to take a slight detour." I asked Roger to take me downtown. We had plenty of time, so he pulled off Route 77 and headed for downtown. Roger asked, "What's up?" I told him to drop me off at the Marine Corps Recruiting Office. His eyebrows went straight up, and he told me my mother was going to kill him. I thought he could be right, but not to worry. "I won't tell her it was you who took me." He said, "I always thought you were nuts, and this proves it." He was just as scared as me. After dropping me off, Roger went on to college. I zoomed into the Marine Corps Recruiters' Office and asked if I could join the Marine Corps for two years. They said, "Yes, we are drafting for two years. Therefore, you could also join for two years." They told me they had one other good thing happening, and if I liked California, I could go there for boot camp instead of Parris Island. I would be a Hollywood Marine. It seemed great, but at the same time, I thought I'd be so far from home. I'd never been across country or flown on an airplane. The Marine recruiters were pushing, and I was listening and finally asked, "Two years and I am out?" They said, "Two years active duty and also four years inactive reserves totaling a six-year obligation. Once done with active duty, there will be no obligation to attend summer camp in the reserves." I said, "Okay, I will join although I don't want to leave just yet." They asked if I wanted to be in their delayed program. I opted for the delayed program.

January 25, 1966 was the date set for me to go to San Diego for boot camp. It seemed like I had a long time between September 1965 and January 25, 1966. I thought it was great because Angela and I were getting tighter every day. I now had a job in the glue division of the Goodyear Tire & Rubber Company with a military obligation in the future. Now

I needed to permanently glue in my relationship with Angela. She was falling in love too. Things were really starting to click, and for sure, I didn't want to leave her, but I had no choice. Everybody was going. I had three buddies who went into the Air Force for four years, and a couple of buddies also went in the Navy for four years. I was going in for two years and out; that's it. In the end, I was only in the Marine Corps for twenty-two months.

Angela was born and raised as a Catholic, a very strict Catholic. We were both virgins when I left, and I could only dream. Before leaving, I asked her to become engaged. She said no! She said I chose to go in the Marine Corps, and I might go off to war, but she would make me a deal. If I came back safe, she would accept my engagement offer. I said, "Deal!" Then after all the going-away parties and goodbyes to friends and relatives, I finally said goodbye to Angela, and off I went.

The president made it clear to the country we needed to stop the spread of Communism (the domino effect) and keep the land of opportunity, the United States of America, free.

At the time of this picture Angela was a senior in high school.

Michael decorating Angela's hair with tinsel on the last Christmas home prior to Vietnam.

(Picture courtesy of Michael Chapanar.)

One year later
Michael was putting up and decorating
a Christmas tree on the DMZ.

(Picture courtesy of Michael Chapanar.)

But first boot camp

Headed for the Marine Corps and the first time ever on an airplane, I arrived at the Marine Corps Recruiting Depot (MCRD) in San Diego on January 25, 1966. The only thing I knew for sure was I needed to adapt and survive. Later I realized boot camp was only a slight preparation for war, and life was about to change forever. There were so many troops moving around, and MCRD was crawling with guys who resembled maggots from wearing a USMC hat (cover) all day in sunny San Diego. It seemed, whatever you needed to do, you had to wait in line at attention. My first haircut took a minute and a half to completely shave my head bald, but the waiting in line at attention to get a haircut seemed like hours. Just a few days in the sun gave you a great tan on your face and ears, yet the whole top of your head was still white. For this reason, Marine Corps drill instructors referred to us as maggots. "Okay, maggots, let's move!"

CHAPTER 7

A Sweetheart's Candy

Everything at boot camp was going well, and I was not singled out or reprimanded for anything yet. It was coming up on Valentine's Day, and both drill instructors were tough and no-nonsense. One day mail call was announced, and one of the drill instructors would always feel your envelope to see if anything strange was in it. My loving little Angela sent me a heart-shaped mint that read, "I love you." It was in my envelope. The drill instructor Sgt. Knott yelled out, "Private Chapanar!" then tossed the envelope down on the deck and said, "Just stand there, maggot, you'll get your mail later." After mail call was finished, I was told to open up the letter, and I found the heart-shaped mint. The DI frowned and sarcastically said, "Oh, ain't that sweet. She sent it to you, so go ahead and eat it." I replied, "Sir, Private Chapanar does not want to eat pogey bait (candy), sir." He replied, "Eat it." I again replied, "Yes, sir" and ate it. He asked if I enjoyed my sweet treat. I replied, "Private Chapanar did not enjoy his pogey bait, sir." He then said, "Too bad! You'll have to do some work now to burn off the sugar." I yelled back, "Yes, sir!" All night long I was digging holes. When I got one hole dug, a DI would come along and ask, "What are you doing digging a hole and putting the dirt over here? Put that dirt back in the hole, and dig a hole over there." I put the dirt back in the hole and dug another hole over there.

Another DI would then come along and say, "What the hell are you doing putting that dirt in my hole? Dig that hole out, put that dirt over here." I did this all night long for a little piece of Angela's candy. Angela didn't know what she did would cause me so much grief. I wrote and told her to never send me anything in boot camp again. *No! No! Never!*

Before joining the corps, the digging-holes bit was something all future boot recruits heard about. I promised myself that I would never do anything in boot camp that would have me digging holes all night. I didn't. Angela did!

The "candy heart" debacle.

CHAPTER 8

Popeye's Olive Oyl

Things went well after that grueling night. I graduated from boot camp and went on to infantry training regiment (ITR) for six weeks and then home for a thirty-day furlough. I came home and looked ridiculous with a white head and no hair. I had no hair on the sides and a few sprouts of hair on top of my head. Angela never visualized me looking like a maggot, and she was totally bewildered at my appearance. But I was home. I brought a friend home with me whom I had met in boot camp. His name was Willard, and he was drafted into the Marine Corps. He lived in California, and prior to being in the military,

Willard loved going up and down the Pacific Coast Highway in his Corvette convertible. He would always tell us about the girls he picked up and the fun he had. Willard had never been out of the state of California and heard Ohio was green, plush, and beautiful. He wanted to come to Ohio and see what it was like for a week.

I introduced him to Angela. Angela was very petite with thin legs and arms and had big, brown eyes with beautiful dark hair— sound familiar? When I introduced her, I noticed Willard had a sour look on his face. As we walked away, he said, "Hey, why don't you ditch Olive Oyl and come on out to California, and I'll show you some real girls with blond hair and blue eyes (California girls)?" I asked him, "What did you call her?"

He said, "Olive Oyl, you know, Popeye's Olive Oyl! It's what she looks like!" I said, "You're crazy, man, she's really cute."

He agreed that she was cute, but asked, "What about the rest of her? She's a stick figure. She looks just like Olive Oyl." I said, "She would fill out, and all I care about are her pretty face and personality." Willard remarked, there were a million girls out there, and I needed to go to California and meet some of these California babes. Willard didn't particularly care for Angela's thin body. One night, Angela and I were together, and I made the mistake of telling her what Willard had said, calling her Olive Oyl. That was it; from that night on she hated Willard. She also didn't want me to meet California babes (blond-haired, blue-eyed California girls). Angela was probably a little intimidated, but the reason she did not like Willard was because he had named her Olive Oyl. In Angela's eyes that was embarrassing and a disgrace, not complimentary whatsoever (her words, not mine).

After my thirty-day leave, I was sent down to Camp Lejeune to learn our military occupation specialty (MOS)—our jobs in the Marine Corps. Willard and I, along with a few guys from Ohio, were in the same platoon. We all became MOS 1371 combat engineers. We were learning how to blow up and destroy things with explosives. We were not the kind of engineers who worked with heavy equipment, built, or constructed anything. Our specialty was explosives, putting in and taking out mines and blowing up everything in sight we could put our hands on.

It was what our group was taught to do as 1371 combat engineers. We were at Camp Lejeune for about five weeks. Camp Lejeune was eleven hours away from Ohio by car.

On Friday's at four thirty it was like the Indianapolis 500. Everyone was trying to leave the base at the same time. We ran to our cars for the eleven-hour daunting drive home.

I would arrive home around three thirty or four in the morning and would throw pebbles at Angela's bedroom window on the second floor to wake her up. The car we drove home was completely rusted out. It was a 1959 Chevy, and in Ohio a car would rust out quickly. It was rusted out so badly, I had to put paving bricks on each side of the radiator to prevent it from hitting the fan blades. In the back seat I put a wood board across the floor as there was a fifteen-inch hole rusted out, and a passenger's feet could fall through the hole. The frame was partially rusted, and the floorboard was completely rusted out as well. We would pile five or six Marines in my classic ride and head north up the road. Eleven hours later we were home. We made this trip five weeks in a row.

One time, we were on our way home when my buddy Gem fell asleep in the back seat with his feet resting on top of the passenger's front seat. Suddenly, his feet slipped down to the floor. The thin board broke, and his feet went through the floorboard. At first I thought he was joking, but the soles of his boots were actually dragging on the pavement. I was traveling about sixty-five miles per hour and had to slowly stop the car. Fortunately, he did not lose his feet or toes. It turned out to be one of the funniest things to happen in the Marine Corps, but not at the time.

Four or five weeks later, during one of our five weekly trips, we were on our way home again, and everything was going smoothly. We were traveling through Breezewood, Pennsylvania, about three-fourths the way home, when I heard a clunk and felt something shift. The bricks shifted, causing the radiator to slide back and hit the fan blades.

You know the saying, "when shit hits the fan"? The radiator hit the fan, and the fan blades broke off and flew straight through the hood of the car, clean through the hood like shrapnel. It looked like someone took a can opener to the hood. Gem was sitting in the front seat and said, "Hey, how about that, what the hell just happened here? Did this piece of crap blow a rod or something?" I didn't know what to say although it didn't seem to slow the car down at first. I was not sure if we would make it home, and I didn't know what the hell happened to my hood! Gem said, "Just don't stop." Then we started to flame out. The car was spewing smoke and steam as pieces were grinding off, and debris was flying in all directions. People were gawking as they tried to get around us. It was a spectacle, trying to keep this heap on the road. We were losing water, the engine was heating up, and the car was slowing down from sixty to fifty to forty to thirty. All of a sudden, that's all she wrote, and it froze up.

I struggled to steer the car off to the side of the road.

I was paid twenty dollars for that car also, and it was towed to the junkyard in Breezewood, Pennsylvania. I called my friend Mickey who was home and had not yet left for the Air Force. I told him we were stranded in Breezewood, Pennsylvania, and he needed to come pick us up. He thought I was joking, but he came down in his dad's new car. We ended up having a beautiful ride home. This debacle was another one of the funniest things that happened while in the Marine Corps, but not at the time! We would always head back to Camp Lejeune on Sunday afternoon, around 3:30 p.m., in order to get back to the base for reveille at 4:30 a.m. on Monday.

It's hard to understand how tired we were from these weekend trips. When Monday morning rolled around, we were fortunate to get back on time. Reveille would blow, and our day would start. We were so tired at the end of the day, we could barely function. We would do our week's training and destroy everything we could find with eyes on Friday, knowing we were going home again. Gem ended up bringing his own '57 Chevy back to the base the following week.

Meanwhile, Angela had graduated from high school and was now working at American Electric Power (AEP). She thought, *No problem, Michael will be home for the weekend*, and she never realized how hectic these trips were for us Marines. We were on the road, totaling twenty-two hours to be home for thirty-six hours at most, but we made the long haul almost every weekend. We had four or five Marines from Canton in the car most of the time. I had to get home to see Angela and could not pass up the opportunity being so close to Ohio. Once we got home, it was fun, and we had a blast. But we knew we had to go back. Our trips and training at Camp Lejeune lasted for six weeks. Five weekends we made it home. When the MOS 1371 combat-engineer training ended, we were given two weeks' leave, and that's when I took Angela to her senior prom. I realized that was about it as the war was blazing big time. We were then sent back to Camp Pendleton, California, knowing we would be getting orders to Vietnam soon.

CHAPTER 9

Not Just Another Brick in the Wall

I needed to take something with me into the Marine Corps and eventually to Vietnam—something visual that would keep my mind calm, some item or thing I could concentrate on at the worst of times, an item with no emotion attached to it. One night while sitting in Angela's living room, I was staring at her living-room fireplace, and it jumped out at me. It was the third brick down on the right side of the fireplace. I thought if, somehow, I could get back home in one piece and see that particular brick again, all would be okay. I would again be home in her living room, and there would be a good chance we would still be in love. Seeing the third brick down again would mean to me that everything worked out, and we would be forever together just like the brick.

The third brick down became a focus point for me when things got tough. My mind would always take me back to that particular brick. Unemotional and real, the brick was rough, strong, hard, cemented in, and exactly where I needed it to be—Angela's living room. It was the way I needed to roll. Seeing the third brick down again was always included in my thoughts and prayers.

CHAPTER 10

North Island Nuclear Weapon Training Center

In July of '66 we were sent back to Camp Pendleton in Southern California. The USMC put us on a new and final phase of training for war called lock-on training. The days consisted of war games to simulate all the possible things we might experience in Vietnam. There were times when you were able to get away for the weekend. Occasionally, during lock-on training, you would get off at 4:30 p.m. on Fridays and would not have to be back until 4:30 a.m. on Monday morning unless you pulled guard duty or had other projects going on. I would head to Oceanside, to a particular bar, play records on the juke-box, sit around with the rest of the homesick Marines, and have a few beers, telling stories and wishing we were home.

One Sunday night, I had been at the bar since about 3:00 p.m. I frequented this bar four or five times in the past. Growing up, I was not a drinker, but on this particular day, I found out what the *sauce* was all about. About 10:00 p.m., three MPs walked in the door and yelled out, "Is Lance Corporal Michael Chapanar in here?" The bartender knew who I was and pointed his index finger directly at me from behind the bar. Two of the three MPs approached and said, "Lance Corporal Chapanar, you are to come with us. We have your seabag packed, we have your gear packed, and we have it all in the car outside."

I could not imagine what this was about. They said, "You are going to San Diego North

Island Naval Air Station on a bus for temporary duty." I was dumbfounded! "North Island?" I asked. "Might there be a prison out there like Alcatraz?" They said, "No, you are going down to the naval air station. We don't know why, but we are to put you on a bus, and you are going to San Diego, to the end of Main Street, where a Navy boat will be waiting for you. They'll take you over to North Island Naval Air Station." I said, "I am not in tip-top shape at the moment." They asked, "How were you going to get back to the base?" I replied, "I would take a cab or go back with another Marine. How can I go to San Diego like this?" They said, "Marine, you don't have a choice. You are going to North Island." I fell asleep on the bus, and next I knew, I was in San Diego. I had my seabag over my shoulder, and I was walking in circles and sideways down to the pier. I reached the pier and gave the Navy boys my papers, and they told me to get my ass on the boat!

I was inebriated, and the boat was bobbing up and down in the ocean. So the Navy boys gave me the ultimate ride. They detected I was probably a little under the influence, so they had some fun and made a few unnecessary maneuvers to give me a little extra ride. I could tell these Navy guys were doing stupid things with the boat and laughing. It was the Navy being the Navy. When we pulled ashore, I met another Navy dude who was waiting to escort me to the barracks. I was feeling a little woozy at the time when I asked if there was a nearby head (restroom) in the area. I strolled into the head and puked my guts out.

It was pretty late, about 1:30 or 2:00 a.m. My escort took me on to the barracks, and the next thing I knew, I closed my eyes, and reveille sounded. A sergeant came in and said, "All you guys come with me." I went with him to smell breakfast then to a classroom where a lieutenant colonel entered. He said, "We have a volunteer mission, and you guys all volunteered." I was wondering what I volunteered for this time. I volunteered to join the Marine Corps, and at lock-on training, they asked if we were all volunteers for Vietnam. You had to be an oddball to say no. So you ended up volunteering for Vietnam, and now you're in a building where a lieutenant colonel was telling you about a volunteer mission with a tactical nuclear weapon. He said, "Look, if anybody wants to get up now and walk out, no harm, no foul. You can go back to your original unit. So are we all volunteers or not?" Everyone was looking around, perplexed with blank looks on their faces. I figured, what were the chances of learning to work a nuclear weapon and strapping it on then having to blow it off? This had to be like a million-to-one shot. I was in disbelief. Less than a year and a half ago, I was playing baseball and not thinking of anything, but Angela and baseball. There was no war going on that I knew of at the time. Now they're talking about strapping a nuclear weapon on my body and having me carry this thing into a battlefield.

What were the chances of getting away from it before it went off? They're going to drop you out of an airplane or helicopter and, somehow, get you to the target zone. If you jumped from an aircraft with the bomb, you would then reach a set altitude and pull the bomb-release strap, letting it tether away, landing just prior to your own landing. You could not dream this stuff up. Some of this training involved Navy personnel, yet I didn't join the Navy. At the time, the Navy boys were nicknamed and referred to as UDT or frogmen. When the initial ten-day Atomic Demolitions Munitions School

(ADMS) training period was over, you were a 1372 MOS ADM technician in addition to your being an original MOS 1371 combat engineer.

On the first day after our morning briefing, we were confirmed as official volunteers to become (1372s) atomic demolition employment techs. We broke up into small groups and were taken to various Quonset hut offices. I remember waiting in a room to be interviewed, and I was last in my group to be called in. It was a job interview with no written résumé.

A lieutenant colonel called me into his office, and I was instructed to sit down and relax. He and two others in the room needed to go over various items and would be asking several questions. I didn't think it would take that long. The Marines ahead of me took ten or fifteen minutes each.

The interview began innocently enough with questions on how I felt about the Marine Corps to this point. They alluded to what I thought of my training to date, and did the training live up to my expectations? Then came questions about the Corps and how I felt about my commanders and various experiences. I was told to speak freely and openly, and nothing said would leave the room or be held against me. I had nothing negative to say about the U.S. Marine Corps.

I could see they had an open file on the desk. They began asking personal questions and were reading the questions from a file folder. When they asked me about changing transmissions in a car I previously owned, I knew they were fully aware of my past, including the make and model of the cars I had owned. He wanted to know how I changed out an automatic transmission and put in a stick shift on my own with no help. I explained I did it in four days on the side of my mom's house in shade on a grassy area. I jacked the car up and put it on cement blocks with the front end slightly higher than the back end. The automatic transmission weighed more than two hundred pounds and was awkward to handle while on your back under the car. I removed a lot of bolts and linkage then slid the transmission back onto a couple of two-by-twelve planks, which were on top of several round pipes I used as rollers. I pulled the planks out from under the car with a rope and removed the transmission. I torched out a hole in the floor for the four-speed stick-shift handle and welded in a clutch-pedal assembly on the left of the brake pedal. Then I reassembled the new used flywheel, clutch plate, and yoke and slid the four-speed standard ninety-pound transmission back into position. I told the lieutenant colonel I had a paperback manual and a telephone number to the junkyard. I had to call the junkyard for advice a few times. When I started the car up and put it in gear and let out the clutch, the wheels started turning. It surprised me, it worked. I lowered the car off the cement blocks, backed it up onto the street, and drove off.

I had no help other than over the phone, and it was the first time I ever did any mechanical work on an automobile. The lieutenant colonel asked me if I knew Dottie and Bill Ryan. I told him Bill and Dottie were my mom's friends and neighbors who lived across the street at the time. He said, "Bill and Dottie informed us about the transmission change."

I looked at the file on his desk. It was thick, and I realized they had more than a résumé for this interview.

This was no ordinary job interview, and it was not any ordinary job.

They proceeded to question me about weird things and thoughts. How did I feel about the war? How did I feel about religion? Had I ever thought or dreamed of being a hero? How would I handle the aftermath of killing human beings? What would it take in my mind to kill another human being? Did I have any regrets in life up to this point? How would I react if someone was going to take the life of a family member or friend, and I had the ability to stop the event? What would I be willing to sacrifice in order to save our country?

The meeting was getting lengthy, and no one else had previously spent this much time answering questions. I was beginning to think this lieutenant colonel was a psychologist although he had no medical insignias.

The lieutenant colonel was aware both my father, Paul Chapanar, and mother were of full Romanian descent with their families being immigrants from Romania. He also knew everything about my family's military service—Mother and Father serving in the United States Navy, Uncle George's service in the U.S. Army in World War I, Uncle John Chapanar's service in the U.S. Army in World War II, including my uncle, Lt. Col. Emil Chapanar, USAFR, Ret., and his son, retired military, Lt. Col. Lawrence Emil Chapanar, USAFR.

Then they asked me several mind-boggling questions, such as the following: When was the last time I had seen or spoken to John Paul Vann? What was John Paul Vann like? Did I respect him? Did I like him? He continued on, asking me if I would rather be a well-decorated Marine hero who was killed in action, saving his country from defeat, or be an ordinary citizen living an ordinary, uneventful life? I replied, "I'd rather be an ordinary citizen home with my girlfriend and playing baseball. I joined the Marine Corps for two years to get in, serve my country, and get out, not to get killed." The session ended with the question of why I joined the Marine Corps.

CHAPTER 11

The Training Begins

The remainder of the day was spent watching films and reviewing itineraries about the up-and-coming next nine days.

The day ended at dinner that evening, and I was informed several Marines at the morning briefing washed out and were sent back to their original unit at Camp Pendleton. When a Marine was given the private opportunity to back out of this volunteer duty, he did just that. Now there were twelve of us left.

The initial ten-day training at North Island Nuclear Weapons Training Center encompassed the following to the best of my recollection:

Intro into Destructive Impact—Uses and scenarios

Intro into Conditions—Exposure, safety, and surviving the blast

Intro into Methods of Deployment and Target Zones—Illustrated with several films

Intro into Locks and Safety Systems—Dimensions and weights, bomb components, including parts and names, arming and disarming the bomb

Intro into Destruction Detonation of the Weapon—Other than as a nuclear explosion

Intro into All Equipment— Needed to carry out a successful strike

Classes and Techniques— Staying calm with maximum focus and concentration under pressure and time constraints

Intro into Communication— Morse code, communication devices, and commands

Intro into Casing Straps and Harnesses

Intro into Strapping on the Bomb—Fasteners, flotation devices, parachuting, tethering, cold-water training, device failures, rehearsals, and drills. Most of the day

was done with reel-to-reel
film put up on a screen like
a movie.

It was a lot to learn in ten days, and I had
no way of knowing it was just the beginning.
The last day of training at North Island, San
Diego, included a debriefing. The commanders were adamant about combat experience
being the next step. Training was useful, but
combat experience was a necessary element
in moving forward with the "atomic demolition munition" process. I was scheduled to
go to Vietnam within a few weeks and was
informed that when I had some combat time
under my belt, I would possibly hear back
from them.

I understood they weren't interested in
going forward without knowing how I would
handle decision-making and composure in
battle. The mission required a proven depend-
able person in action. I had not yet been

proven, and there was no substitute for combat. Playing war games at Camp Pendleton proved nothing.

The training and debriefing ended with a sermon on how airtight and secret the project had to be. Trustworthiness and keeping it airtight were paramount.

We were assured we would be tested. Any leaking of information would result in washing out of the program and severe punishment, possibly the brig. I understood leaking was a serious breach.

After the ten-day training was over, I was sent back to my unit at Camp Pendleton; I could not tell a soul what I had been doing or my new MOS. People in my original unit wanted to know where I had been for ten days. I could only say, "It is classified."

Being ferried by helicopter from one part of the Camp Pendleton base to another for a drill with a simulated nuclear weapon was a frequent occurrence. They would always take me to a part of the base away and out of sight of other Marines.

Michael waiting to be whisked off by chopper for a nuclear-weapon-deployment rehearsal and drill at another location on the base.

(Picture courtesy of Michael Chapanar.)

CHAPTER 12

A Character

One characteristic exhibited was the ability to focus and make good decisions under harsh conditions. It was discovered by the U.S. Marine Corps that I was at peak proficiency when put in dire situations. I could focus in the most trying settings the Marine Corps and Navy put upon me.

While at San Diego North Island Naval Air Station they actually tried to drown me for clowning around in the swimming pool. With leg strength and endurance, I could swim well and stay afloat like a frog, not giving up regardless of how many weights they tried putting on me. I'd find a way out and survive the exercise. Unbeknownst to me, a swimming instructor pretended to be a recruit drowning in the pool. At the time, I was completely exhausted when, out of the corner of my eye, I saw this so-called recruit drowning. With a second wind I swam over to him. He grabbed on to me, pretending to save himself, and we both went underwater. I couldn't get another breath of air, so I wrapped my legs around him in a scissors-leg-and-choke hold. When he stopped struggling, I dragged him to the edge of the pool. He had passed out, but the other drill instructors thought he was still pretending. He was unconscious, and they had to revive him.

After regaining consciousness, one of the drill instructors turned to me and said, "You are quite a character."

The DI could not understand how this could happen to one of his strapping swimming instructors.

I was thinking, if he was still alive, I had done something good by saving him, only to find out I almost killed a DI pretending to be drowning.

I found out early on, the more extremely dangerous the situation, the more I focused. After the military, activities like solo skydiving and piloting airplanes exposed this characteristic in civilian life as well. I knew this skill would help me in Vietnam. There was no explanation for this unique ability other than a massive desire to get home and see the third brick down again. I realized you must always stay calm and find a way to survive. You just figure it out and keep going!

After North Island I returned to Camp Pendleton to complete lock-on training. Every now and then a high-ranking, non-commissioned officer would order me off to a faraway building where we would practice drills with a simulated nuclear weapon.

We would go through endless checklists and drills for hours. Again, I couldn't tell anybody where I went off to or what we were doing. It happened time and time again.

You knew the Marine Corps was figuring out you might be the guy strapping on the bomb. Early on in boot camp the drill instructors observed the leg strength, and during lock-on training, they had me squatting over four hundred eighty pounds. I was six feet, one hundred seventy pounds, and squatting that much weight was in a class of its own. The obstacle course was one hundred yards long and deep with sand when they ordered us to do a fireman's carry with a fellow Marine. The drill instructor observed I was not a fast runner, but wanted to see how much endurance I could muster up carrying a couple hundred pounds. I would approach one end of the obstacle course when the DI would turn me around and send me back to the other end. I would go to the opposite end again, carrying a two-hundred-pound Marine, and it was a demonstration of endurance. I believe my leg strength and endurance were another reason the Navy continued a background security clearance investigation while still in boot camp.

A few months later, upon finding out I was superclean, I was given a security clearance. The next thing I knew, three MPs were putting me on a bus to San Diego Naval Air Station Nuclear Weapons Training Center, and that's how it all started.

I was very good in boot camp at pugilistic fighting with boxing gloves on both ends of a stick, and nobody knocked me off my feet. In all the fights at the Marine Corps Recruit Depot, no one knocked me down. If needed, I would capture them in a scissors hold, and when they tried to pry my legs off, I would go for their throat, eyes, and ears. I could also apply a choke hold and pull a recruit's neck off his shoulders while squeezing out his breath in a scissors hold. The opponent couldn't breathe and would either tap out or pass out, and the DI would rap me in the head and yell, "Stop!" No one was ever able to free themselves. One Marine actually volunteered, allowing for the scissors hold to be put on him as he was sure he could break the hold. The Marine ended up passing out with broken ribs! I was thinking I might go to the brig for destruction of government property. The scissors hold was nick-named the anaconda snake hold by the drill instructor after this incident. These were just a few more reasons why the USMC concluded I might be the one to carry the bomb.

It really started with riding a bicycle ten miles round trip (fifty miles a week) for years to baseball practice. Bicycle riding to practices and games over the years, combined with being a garbageman carrying thousands of galvanized garbage cans to and from the garbage truck, built my leg strength and endurance. Martial arts and the Marine Corps built up the legs further with heavyweight squatting. I was totally unaware they were formulating a plan to use my legs on the battlefield with a ninety-pound backpack nuke.

CHAPTER 13

A South Pacific Cruise

Our Eleventh Engineer Combat Battalion knew the cruise to Vietnam was coming; we just didn't know when the boat was leaving. In November of 1966, the battalion was bused from Camp Pendleton to Long Beach, California, and we were shipped out to Vietnam aboard the *U.S.S. Okanogan*.

It was very close living quarters for thirty days aboard a transport ship with about one thousand four hundred military personnel aboard. I was sick only once, and that's when a Marine threw up on me. On November 10 we docked at Pearl Harbor; it was the Marine Corps's birthday. Two days later, after a brief celebration, we were out to sea again, and the Navy set up a small boxing ring on the top deck of the ship. A naval officer instructed the Marines to round up their best boxers. They called the boxing matches smoker bouts—the Marine boys against the Navy men as they put it.

I was chosen to fight and faced a tough test. My opponent was an undefeated Hispanic, and there was betting going on. The fight was three rounds lasting three minutes per round. I figured I had little chance of beating this sailor. He had been boxing on the ship for almost a year, and I was not really a boxer. Every time they picked up a new load of Marines, this sailor was in the smokers.

I was doing okay in the first two rounds— the third round, not so much.

This Navy specimen had a great left jab and threw a left hook off his left jab to my jaw. He also had a good right uppercut, and he nailed me. I just about went down while keeping my head low, still bobbing and weaving and half out on my feet. Staying low I came up with a punch of my own. I quickly rose up to throw an uppercut, and his chin was directly above my head. The top of my head hit the underside of his jaw, and it happened so fast, everyone thought I nailed him with a right uppercut. I knew I got him with the top of my head, and my uppercut whizzed past his jaw. I just grazed him with my glove, and it was my head that knocked him out. He went down for the count, and the fight was over. I won by a stroke of luck, using my head.

The ship was now sitting off the coast of Vietnam. No lights or smoking were permitted on the top deck, and we were just several miles offshore and south of the DMZ. You could easily hear the guns going off and the sounds of war rumbling. We could see the night-illumination flares lighting up the Vietnam coastline. We were waiting for the sea to calm so we could go ashore. One night, after waiting for over a week, we thought we heard two jets flying over the ship and what sounded like explosions. We then heard the ship's emergency horn and felt the prop turning. It was determined, what sounded like jets were actually two artillery shells being fired at us from deep inside North Vietnam. We quickly sailed farther out to sea and out of range after undergoing our first combat action of war.

CHAPTER 14

Signatures Required

The first six weeks in Vietnam I was, in fact, battle tested on the DMZ and found to be a person who could keep composure. On January 17, 1967, the battalion commander Lieutenant Colonel Mulford pulled me out of field combat and back to the Dong Ha base. He asked me to sign a document (reliability screening certificate) while also explaining I would not be receiving a promotion from the rank of lance corporal to corporal while in Vietnam. He went on to say I would not be taking on any responsibilities of other Marine personnel, and a promotion was not necessary in light of my 1372 ADM duties. The absence of a promotion was confusing and frustrating although the lieutenant colonel said I could expect a promotion upon return to the United States.

The U.S. Department of Defense Nuclear Personnel Reliability Program (PRP) is a security, medical, and psychological evaluation program. Its purpose is to permit only the most trustworthy individuals to have access to nuclear weapons.

According to the *Department of Defense Manual* only those personnel who had demonstrated the highest degree of individual reliability for allegiance, trustworthiness, conduct, behavior, and responsibility shall be allowed to perform duties associated with nuclear weapons, and they shall be continuously evaluated for adherence to NPRP standards. The Nuclear Personnel Reliability Program evaluated many aspects of the individual's work life and homelife.

A transcription of the document I signed read as follows: "I have been briefed on, and understand the spirit and intent of MCO 5510.7, and aware of the **SERIOUSNESS** of the duties which I have been assigned, and recognize the need for **DEPENDABILITY** in my assignment."

The battalion commanding officer Lt. Col. Mulford's signature acknowledged the following: "The individual named above has been qualified to occupy a reliability billet (including special security clearance housing in Okinawa) and has been briefed by me regarding the **IMPORTANCE** and **SERIOUSNESS** of his duties."

* * *

Upon leaving the commander's tent on this bleak day in January, my emotions ran wild. The conversation that preceded the signing and the repercussions I felt became a heavy burden on my shoulders. I felt, in a way, I was given a death sentence and unable to tell a soul about it. I knew in Col. Mulford's tone, as he was explaining to me the extreme situation, that it was just as devastating to him. It was hard for me to imagine how I was taking on such an important role in history. The unimaginable was now a reality. It took me a few hours to emotionally recover from this meeting.

Michael Paul Chapanar LCPL MOS 1372
Reliability Screening Certificate
signed January 17, 1967

HEADQUARTERS
11th Engineer Battalion
Fleet Marine Force, Pacific
FPO San Francisco 96602

SRB
Copy

RELIABILITY SCREENING CERTIFICATE

Ref: MCO 5510.7

Michael Paul CHAPANAR	LCPL	/1372
(NAME)	(GRADE)	(SER NO/MOS)

I have been briefed on, and understand the spirit and intent of MCO
5510.7, am aware of the seriousness of the duties which I have been
assigned, and recognize the need for dependability in my assignment.

Michael P. Chapanar   Jan 17, 1967
(Signature)   (Date)

The individual named above has been found qualified to occupy a
reliability billet and has been briefed by me regarding the importance
and seriousness of his duties.

R. L. MULFORD, LtCol
(Signature and Grade)

Commanding Officer
(Title)   (Date)

- -
II

Type Billet Assigned __Limited__   Security Clearance __SECRET__
                    (Date)   (Date)
Medical Record Checked __1Jan67__   Service Record Checked __1Jan67__
                    (Date)   (Date)
NAC Completed __9Mar66__   BI Completed _____
                    (Date)   (Date)
- -
III

Denial/Termination Data: 22 Nov 1967
                                              (Date)

1. Explain reasons or circumstances in brief narrative form.

2. Attach supporting documents (medical eval., board results,
   statements, etc.) as appropriate.

3. Use reverse side if necessary.

Copy to: OQR/SRB (Original), CMC (Code DGH) (Duplicate)
         (Others, as locally required)

Case File #
c/c SS 24 379 658

145

CHAPTER 15

The First of Three Nuclear Weapon Assignments to Okinawa

Approximately one week after signing the reliability screening certificate, I was summoned out of the field again and ordered back to the Dong Ha Combat Base. Upon arrival I scurried to the battalion commander's office. The clerk handed me a sealed envelope. It was orders to go to Okinawa for atomic demolition munitions advanced training (ADM training.)

In a way this was a good thing. I would be out of the war for ten days. After a month and a half of combat on the DMZ, I could hardly wait for the next two days to pass, and I would be out of Vietnam. I found it hard to believe I was important enough that the Marine Corps was actually taking me out of Vietnam and sending me to Okinawa. All of a sudden it hit me. *What do I say to my platoon and all the Marines here in Dong Ha?* The only thing I could say was I had no idea where I was going or why. At the airstrip I met two of the Marines I had trained with at North Island Nuclear Weapons Training Center in San Diego, and we had not seen one another since. They were just as perplexed as me. It was weird; we couldn't talk to one another about ADM training even though we were together again.

The USMC made a purposeful effort to keep the ADM Marines separated from one another in Vietnam. We were all serving in the same Eleventh Engineer Combat Battalion, but no one remembered setting eyes on one another the past few months. When the jeep picked me up to go to the airstrip, several

Marines in our tent area told me to have a good time on R & R (rest and relaxation.) On the plane ride to Okinawa, we shared a few war stories; we were now combat veterans. Upon arrival at Kadena Air Force Base in Okinawa, the three of us were whisked off to a nearby Marine installation. We were transported to a part of the base that looked evacuated and boarded up. It would be home for the next ten days. Welcome to the beautiful and relaxing island of Okinawa; this was not going to be R & R.

At the briefing and orientation that afternoon, we were told we would be seeing pay phones and pay booths in our travels although any phone calls were strictly prohibited. I was very disappointed realizing I couldn't call home while seeing phones everywhere. It was rousting up some claustrophobic feelings.

First thing the next day I was interviewed by a major. Once again it was a job interview.

The major wanted to know what my feelings were regarding the war and the Marine Corps. He also wanted to know about my combat experiences.

I knew there was a chance I might be playing an important part in the war. I probably told the gung ho major more of what he wanted to hear rather than what I was really thinking about the war. At that point, I had convinced myself I was all in, and I didn't want to screw up.

The ADM training started where we finished up at North Island, San Diego. At the beginning of class, we noticed this major had a fifth of whiskey sitting on a table next to his podium. It was partially hidden by a number of manuals, but we spotted it. During a break we were wondering if the major was possibly an alcoholic although we noticed he didn't take the bottle with him on his break. After the break, we did a refresher review of several systems and watched films. At the end of the day the commander asked if anyone had mastered the Morse code yet. Everyone was staring at one another. After a few seconds I tapped out *yes* (-.-- . ...) on the desk. The commander walked over and handed me the fifth of whiskey. On his way back to his podium, he turned and said, "Don't forget to share that." The whiskey was the reward of the day for having learned Morse code.

Michael holding the reward of the day for learning and remembering Morse code.

(Picture courtesy of Michael Chapanar.)

A beautiful tropical island—Okinawa

The U.S. Marine Corps took me out of combat action in Vietnam and sent me to Okinawa for advanced nuclear weapons training three times for ten days with each trip more advanced and sophisticated than the previous. The third trip included understanding some intelligence reports, and I felt I was finally in the loop.

I was fully trained to nuke the enemy and, possibly, blow myself up at the same time to save a combat base on the DMZ from annihilation. After each trip to Okinawa, I was sent back to Vietnam and once again back into combat operations. After the first trip in January, I had no idea I would be returning for a second time in late April. Finally, during the third trip back in July, I was advised I would be returning for a fourth time in September. The September trip never happened. Instead, in September they built a barbershop next to my tent area in Dong Ha, and I was ordered to cut hair. I suddenly became a barber and was ordered to stay close to the barbershop area at all times as they needed to know my whereabouts 24-7.

I was taken from the Vietnam DMZ and sent to Okinawa three times, and I knew the United States was serious about using a tactical nuclear weapon in Vietnam.

The atomic demolition and munition (ADM) was team training, but also involved some very personal training. Not everyone was involved in one-on-one personal training, and as far as I knew, it was only happening with me.

The team training was learning the various components of the bomb and working to set the bomb off in any conceivable weather condition. It was something we did daily in Okinawa, and the repetition was monotonous. Giant fans blowing on us simulated wind while a water hose was used to simulate rain by squirting water in front of the fans. Flickering light switches simulated lightning and explosions. The blowing air and water were uncomfortably cold. Most of the work was done under our ponchos during these simulated conditions. The noise they piped in was deafening. We were taught how to do our job in many different scenarios.

The first ten days of training in Okinawa were a lot more intense than the training I received at North Island Naval Air Station in San Diego.

After completing all phases of every checklist and certain other procedures were done, we would run out of the building to a distance up to approximately five hundred yards away with an entrenching tool and the aluminum protection blanket we were given to protect our eyes and skin.

We were ordered to quickly dig a trench six feet long, two feet wide, and a foot deep, lie down in the trench, and cover ourselves with the protection blanket.

Supposedly, this would protect us from being vaporized and protect our eyes. Our commanders would sometimes give us a cross-eyed look and a smirk and say, "Don't forget to kiss your ass goodbye."

Classroom training involved the two-man system lock combinations, codes, setting timers, then coordinates, terrain familiarization, communications, and possible escape routes. As far as I knew, I was the only one ordered to attend parachute-jump school although I never got to jump with the bomb package. I practiced jumping out of fixed-wing aircraft at altitude. Jumping out of airplanes is still one of my favorite things to do. To this day, I love to solo skydive. Angela goes shopping to resist all negative thoughts.

Ground school was relentless, and everything had to be memorized until it became second nature. Preparation checklists were endless: Do it and then do the whole thing over and over again. Any mistakes and you would have to do the whole day over again all night. The cold-water training was something I dreaded.

Born and raised in Ohio, I was accustomed to winter, but training in cold water was very hard to endure. Getting your body acclimated to being in cold water was not fun, but I was told it was necessary.

In Okinawa they had great mess halls and hot food, but most of the time we were eating C rations.

If all training went well that day, you might get to go back to the barracks with your buddy and a bottle of Jack Daniels that night. Thank God for Sundays. On Sundays we were given a few hours off to attend church and/or go into town to experience part of Okinawa. I met a lot of Okinawan people, and they were thoughtful, wonderful, and kind people. I especially loved the Okinawan children.

Okinawa-no agreements in writing

The island of Okinawa was protected by neither the constitution of the United States nor that of Japan's. The Pentagon exploited the situation by stockpiling an arsenal of nuclear and chemical weapons there throughout the 1960s. In the '50s and '60s the United States built more than seventy-five installations on the island, and most residents of Okinawa were under the assumption the entire island was a U.S. base. During the Vietnam War, Kadena Air Base was one of the busiest airports in the world. The island was so important to the Pentagon, it prompted the commander of the U.S. Pacific Force in 1965 to declare,

"Without Okinawa, the United States could not continue the war in Vietnam."

At one point during this period of time, the U.S. Military employed over fifty thousand Okinawans.

Behind fellow Marine on the left is the commanders' round Quonset hut. Behind Michael on the right is the boarded-up nuclear weapon training facility.

Bombs away

The term *tactical bomb* as defined by the military is "a bomb used for immediate support of military operations on military targets in ground combat situations and avoiding civilian casualties as much as possible."

The MOAB (acronym for *mother of all bombs*) was the most powerful conventional (non-nuclear) bomb in the American arsenal. The MOAB was the successor to the daisy cutter. The daisy cutter was used in Vietnam operations. The blast radius of the MOAB was approximately one mile wide and, within this one-mile area, would suck out all the air and turn your lungs and head inside out. The MOAB's blast was equivalent to eleven tons of TNT. The daisy cutter and the MOAB were both used in the global war on terror in Afghanistan.

In contrast, the nuclear bomb I was trained to use in Vietnam had an explosive yield equal to one thousand tons of TNT. The bomb's total package weighed close to ninety pounds. Debris from the blast could be sent more than one-half mile into the sky and over one mile from the ground-zero target site, raining down rocks, earth, trees, and red-hot steel for more than a minute after detonation. Unlike the MOAB or daisy cutter, the tactical atomic bomb would create radioactive no-go zones and could be used as a temporary blocking force if needed.

The nuclear weapons I trained on had much lower yields than did the two bombs dropped on Japan although a tactical nuclear weapon detonated in a prime spot under ideal conditions could be just as deadly. Location, conditions, and timing were the keys to a successful mission with a tactical nuclear weapon.

The atomic bomb dropped on Japan's city of Hiroshima on August 6, 1945, nicknamed Little Boy, was equivalent to fifteen thousand tons of TNT. It reduced four square miles of the city to rubble upon detonation killing over eighty thousand people. Ninety thousand to one hundred sixty thousand died within four months.

The bomb dropped on Japan's city of Nagasaki on August 9, 1945, nicknamed Fat Man, was equivalent to twenty thousand tons of TNT, killing forty thousand to seventy-five thousand people with the blast and causing absolute, utter destruction of the city.

The NVA buildup

In October and November of 1967, we were receiving intelligence reports about the NVA massing several divisions of infantry troops in the vicinity of Khe Sanh and around the DMZ. We were also aware that some areas were sparsely populated, and the United States could use devastating force and firepower with little civilian collateral damage in certain areas. It was the head-on battle Westmoreland was looking forward to with a chance to annihilate the enemy who could be vulnerable in fixed positions and in large numbers. The opportunity to finally engage and annihilate the enemy was a long awaited one by the general.

When it came to Khe Sanh, Westmoreland was willing to shove his whole chip stack in.

President Johnson and General Westmoreland understood, an American defeat at Khe Sanh on a grand scale would turn the tables against the war efforts in the eyes of the American people. Signs were pointing to a replay of the French defeat at Dien Bien Phu in 1954. This could never be allowed to happen at Khe Sanh or Con Thien.

The Marines at Khe Sanh needed an ace in the hole and an insurance policy waiting in the wings. Uncontrollable factors, like a surprise attack during unforeseen weather conditions that could hamper U.S. air support, were a deck of cards stacked against the U.S. Marines and Westmoreland.

Although American conventional fire-power was enough to stave off any attack in good weather, General Westmoreland knew the NVA high command was well aware of such factors in planning their attacks. Westmoreland had no choice, but to have a solid insurance policy in his arsenal. A tactical nuclear weapon and me ready to move out in seconds were the insurance policy.

At most the tactical nuclear bomb was less than six hours away in Okinawa, and per-haps, it was less than an hour away on an air-craft carrier sitting off the coast of Vietnam. I believe there were times when the bomb was parked in Dong Ha just minutes away. More so, I believe it was actually strapped to me on one scary night.

Patton's speech

Motivational lectures were an intricate part of ADM training. Looking back and learning about important historical events from the past were Marine Corps methods of motivation. There were only a few times I remember the Marine Corps pointing to an outside source for motivation. We gathered for classroom instruction one morning in Okinawa when a colonel in dress blues with a stack of decorations on his chest in full display walked into the room. Someone yelled, "Attention!" The colonel ordered us to be seated. The colonel then rattled off a motivational speech about World War II. It sticks in my mind to this day. It was totally inspiring and had us ready to run through walls. At the end of his speech the colonel referenced the speech as the one given by General Patton to his men the day before D-Day, June 5, 1944. Most of this great speech ended up twenty-six years later in the 1970 five-star film called *Patton*. The following speech is similar to the Twentieth Century Fox Film Corporation's version of the speech given by actor George C. Scott. As he stood in front of his men, he uttered the following words:

> I want you to remember, that no bastard ever won a war dying for his country. He won it by making the other poor dumb bastard die for his countrymen. All this stuff you've heard about America not wanting to fight and wanting to stay out of the war is a lot of horse dung. Americans tradition-ally love to fight. All real Americans love the sting of battle. When you were kids, you all admired the cham-pion marble shooter, the fastest runner, the big league ball players and the tough-

est boxers. Americans love a winner and will not tolerate a loser. Americans play to win all the time. I wouldn't give a hoot in hell for a man who lost and laughed. That's why Americans have never lost and will never lose a war because the very thought of losing is hateful to Americans. Now, an Army is a team. It lives, eats, sleeps, fights as a team. This individuality stuff is a bunch of crap. The biggest bastards who wrote that stuff about individuality for the Saturday Evening Post don't know anything more about real battle than they do about fornication. Now we have the finest food and equipment, the best spirit and the best men in the world. You know, I actually pity those poor bastards we're going up against, by God I do. We're not just going to shoot the bastards, we're going to cut out their living guts and use them to grease the treads of our tanks. We're going to murder those lousy Hun bastards by the bushel. Now, some of you boys I know are wondering whether or not you will chicken out under fire. Don't worry about it. I can assure you that you will all do your duty. The Nazis are the enemy, wade in to them. Spill their blood, shoot them in the belly. Every man is scared in his first action but you are not all going to die in battle. If any man says he is not scared, he is a goddamn liar. The real hero is the man who fights even though he is scared. The real man never lets his fear of death overpower his honor, his sense of duty to his country, and his man-hood. When you put your hand into a bunch of goo that a moment before was your best friend's face, you'll know what to do! Now there's another thing I want you to remember. I don't want to get any messages saying that we are holding our position.

We're not holding anything, let the Hun do that. We are advancing constantly and we are not interested in holding on to anything except the enemy. We're going to hold on to him by the nose and we're going to kick him in the ass! We're going to kick the hell out of him all the time and we're going to go through him like crap through a goose. Now, there is one thing that you men will be able to say when you get back home. And you may thank God for it. Thirty years from now when you're sitting around your fireplace with your grandson on your knee and he asks you what did you do in the great World War II, you won't have to say, well, I shoveled shit in Louisiana. All right now you sons of bitches, you know how I feel. Oh, I will be proud to lead you wonderful guys into battle anytime and anywhere. That's all.

Twenty-three years after Patton had given his great speech in 1944, it was being used again to motivate some crazy Marines in Okinawa who were headed back to Vietnam. I might add, "It worked!" We stood up and gave the colonel an ovation.

(Top picture) Sunday, July 23, 1967, in Okinawa on a ten-day nuclear weapon training mission, Michael dreaming of Angela.

(Bottom picture) At Camp Pendleton, Michael showing off for Angela with three hundred seventy-five pounds on his shoulders.

(Pictures courtesy of Michael Chapanar.)

Michael's mother, Jeanne; Angela's mother, Lena; and Angela saying hi to a person on the other side of the world.

Michael's mother and two Brothers, Tim and Jeff, saying, "Hi" and "Hurry home."

(Pictures courtesy of Michael Chapanar.)

CHAPTER 16

The Ironing-Board Letter

Angela and I were seriously dating, but not engaged before I left for Vietnam. Like I said, I did ask her if she would like to get engaged before I left for Nam, but she declined. She was only seventeen years old when I left. She felt she had a lot of growing up to do before being engaged to one crazy Marine dude.

The only experience she had around Marines was when I came home from boot camp and then Camp Lejeune every weekend to see her with these crazy Marines I brought home with me. Needless to say, Angela was in no hurry to settle down with a Marine or anyone else.

I must say, she had a bit of a jealous streak in her and did not appreciate any outside competition for her steady boyfriend. We wrote letters to each other weekly, and we also both had reel-to-reel tape recorders to use in order to hear each other's voice.

To my dismay, I found out, a letter I had written to a friend was put in the wrong envelope, and off it went to Angela. The letter I wrote to Angela went off to "Susie" (the fog of war). Angela was heartbroken when she started reading her letter and realized it was not meant for her. She now knew I was writing not only to her but also to an old flame as she saw it. As the story goes, Angela was so upset with me and the wrong letter she received that she walked six miles to her best friend's house and commiserated with her.

Angela felt strongly, she had to lash out and express her hurt feelings to me and wanted me to feel just as bad. She came up with the idea that in her eyes, I was only worthy of a reply letter written on special paper. She vigorously began writing the "Dear John" letter with a felt-tip pen on toilet paper she had rolled out over the ironing board in her bedroom as she cried. She thought it was all I deserved after the snafu with the letters. My letter to an old girlfriend reminisced about things the two of us did when we were together, such as planting a tree together.

While in Ca Lu, living underground and in the heat of battle, mail finally reached our unit. I was excited to finally get some mail. I felt the envelope, and it didn't feel like her other letters. It was very thick with a kind of hard covering around it. When I opened it, I could not believe my eyes. I started to read a twenty-foot letter written on toilet paper. It was shocking, and I was devastated. One look at this letter and every Marine knew I was in trouble. The commanders were concerned the letter would affect my psychological well-being. I had to somehow convince them otherwise.

Eleventh Engineer Battalion Squad taking a break while building underground bunkers at Ca Lu.

Michael taking a break and eating an orange, living underground and putting in mines around the Ca Lu perimeter halfway between Dong Ha and Khe Sanh on Route 9.

(Pictures courtesy of Michael Chapanar.)

Battle Operations and Casualty Count through May 17, 1966

Operation Prairie I

Operation Prairie I took place from December 3, 1966, to January 31, 1967, and was conducted by the Third Marine Division to stop the flow of at least two North Vietnamese Army divisions from entering Quang Tri Province south of the DMZ. Each NVA division was approximately ten thousand men strong. *Our Marine losses in this operation were 239 killed and 1,214 wounded.* Enemy losses amounted to 1,397 killed and 27 captured with thousands more wounded.[2]

Surprisingly, the last week in January, I was summoned out of combat operations and sent to Okinawa for a ten-day nuclear weapon

---

[2] Telfer, Major Gary L., Lieutenant Colonel Lane Rogers, USMC, and V.K. Fleming Jr. "The U.S. Marines in Vietnam: Fighting the North Vietnamese, 1967." Washington, D.C.: History and Museums Division, Headquarters, U.S. Marine Corps, 1984,p.21.

training trip. This was to be the first of three trips to Okinawa for training.

Operation Prairie II

Operation Prairie II took place from March 8, 1967, through March 18, 1967, and was a continuation of Operation Prairie I in the same tactical area to stop the infiltration of the North Vietnamese Army into the south. The enemy 324B Division was a major part of the infiltration taking place. *Resulting losses were 93 Marines killed and 483 wounded.* Enemy losses were 693 North Vietnamese Army soldiers and Viet Cong killed.[3]

---

[3] Telfer, Major Gary L., Lieutenant Colonel Lane Rogers, USMC, and V.K. Fleming Jr. "The U.S. Marines in Vietnam: Fighting the North Vietnamese, 1967." Washington, D.C.: History and Museums Division, Headquarters, U.S. Marine Corps, 1984,p.26.

Operation Prairie III

Operation Prairie III lasted from March 19, 1967, through April 19, 1967. Although lasting until April 19, 1967, I was not personally involved the last three days because of a second nuclear weapon training trip back to Okinawa. This operation was a further continuation of Prairie II to halt ground incursions of NVA into South Vietnam. *U.S. Marine losses were 56 killed with 530 Marines wounded.* Enemy losses amounted to 252 North Vietnamese Army and Viet Cong killed. [4]

Operation Prairie IV

Operation Prairie IV, conducted from April 20, 1967, to May 17, 1967, was carried

---

[4] Telfer, Major Gary L., Lieutenant Colonel Lane Rogers, USMC, and V.K. Fleming Jr. "The U.S. Marines in Vietnam: Fighting the North Vietnamese, 1967." Washington, D.C.: History and Museums Division, Headquarters, U.S. Marine Corps, 1984,p.31.

out in this same small Leatherneck Square area and around Con Thien. Friendly losses *were 164 killed and 1,240 wounded.* The North Vietnamese Army suffered 505 dead.[5] During this time period, on April 16 to the first week in May, I was out of Vietnam for my second nuclear training trip to Okinawa.

---

[5] Telfer, Major Gary L., Lieutenant Colonel Lane Rogers, USMC, and V.K. Fleming Jr. "The U.S. Marines in Vietnam: Fighting the North Vietnamese, 1967." Washington, D.C.: History and Museums Division, Headquarters, U.S. Marine Corps, 1984,p.30.

CHAPTER 17

Reel-to-Reel or Unreal

On the first ten-day ADM training trip to Okinawa in January, I purchased two tape recorders and sent one home to Angela. Now, Angela and I both had our own reel-to-reel tape recorders. They both were the same make and model, battery operated.

I had to turn the reel with my finger when batteries were low, and her voice would go high or low, fast or slow, depending on how steady you could turn the reel. It was hard to understand the words. She would sound like Donald Duck then, like a very low-voiced man. When you turned the reel just right, it sounded like Angela's beautiful voice. It was hard to do just right.

I knew I was in trouble and had to get a letter and explanation off to Angela fast. This other girl, Susie, was a friend, not a girlfriend. I had to convince Angela that Susie was just a friend, using a three-week delayed mail system from nine thousand miles away—not an easy task while hunkered down and dodging bullets.

Our platoon could not believe I had this reel-to-reel, battery-operated tape recorder. My claustrophobia feelings were at an all-time high. I thought if I was lucky, I would get a letter and answer back in about six weeks—that is, if I still had any chance with Angela. Being out in the field away from Dong Ha, receiving incoming artillery, and living underground at Ca Lu surrounded by enemy forces were not exactly on the direct daily-mail route.

Within two weeks and before she received my apology letter and explanation, she sent me a tape. She must have really felt bad about sending the toilet-paper letter.

The batteries in my recorder were now completely dead. I had no way of listening to it. It would not make a sound even if you turned it with your finger. The batteries were done. I didn't know who, but someone sent for batteries from Dong Ha. I never did know who sent for the batteries. One night, the new batteries just showed up on my cot. We were using candlelight, living underground, and out of nowhere was Angela's voice. She was actually saying there was still a chance for us if I would quit writing Susie. Susie never received another letter! Susie kept writing, but I never answered. The rest was history. I was sure my commanders began to relax. I would not be surprised if it was the ADM commander or CIA who sent for the new batteries. After all, they had to keep me from cracking up.

CHAPTER 18

Out of Country

In April of 1967, I hitched a ride by chopper up to Con Thien. My assignment was to help put in and lay down mines around the out-skirts of the firebase perimeter.

They needed to bolster and upgrade the barrier already set in place around the Con Thien area with additional claymore anti-personnel land mines. I did not mind this work because it kept me pretty close to the compound and not someplace far out in the wilderness. When enemy artillery would hit the base, I was usually far enough out that it kind of put me in a safe zone. The real worry was sniper fire. At the end of the day, I was sore from crawling around, and my knees were taking a beating. I had to stay as low as possible and out of sight from enemy snipers. They would shoot at us several times a day; I suspect they just wanted to let us know they were there.

At the farthest point out, I was installing and mapping the victim-activated version of these claymore mines. Most were activated by trip wire and some by pressure switch. When activated, the claymore, which resembled a Polaroid camera case, would, in a way, take your last picture. It would flash like a flashbulb in a camera, and at the same time the explosive detonation would blast out about six hundred or seven hundred steel balls at whoever tripped the wire. The effective kill range was thirty to fifty meters and would pan out twenty-five to thirty degrees to either side of the center aiming target sight. If you were close enough and tripped the wire or activated the pressure switch, you were also dead.

Closer in on the perimeter and around our barbed-wire barriers, we would set the electronic detonation version of this directional fragmentation mine. The command detonation electronic version allowed the operator total control of the timing of detonation. You could detonate these devices at the most lethal exact time, and there was very little worry an animal would inadvertently set one off.

One month later, Con Thien was attacked in the early-morning hours on May 8. I was in Dong Ha at the time of the attack on Con Thien and had just returned from my second nuclear training assignment in Okinawa. We received word of the attack in Dong Ha, and we were being bombarded with artillery at the same time. We heard the brutal attack on Con Thien was bad, but the outpost survived.

It was the thirteenth anniversary of the fall of Dien Bien Phu. The North Vietnamese Army attempted to pull off another Dien Bien Phu and overrun the entire firebase although with not enough firepower or men, this time ending in failure.

The enemy breached the barriers and the defensive barbed wire with bangalore torpedoes. They were also armed with flamethrowers and rocket-propelled grenades. Enemy soldiers entered the perimeter, and hand-to-hand combat was inevitable. Some of our Eleventh Engineer boys inside moved over to the breached perimeter to help fend off the onslaught and reinforce that particular area. The fight lasted from 3:00 a.m. until after daylight.

Enemy soldiers were carrying satchel charges and exploding them under our Marine vehicles inside the perimeter. On this night, forty-four Marines were killed, and one hundred ten were wounded. We heard a total of twenty-seven of our Eleventh Engineer Battalion Combat Marines were hurt, but none were killed on scene. I didn't know if any of them died.

Upon my return from Okinawa, the guys were asking me where I disappeared to. Obviously, I could not tell them why I was gone or what I was doing. Some guys who knew I was out of Vietnam thought I was out of the country, having a good time. If I could have only told them I was being trained with a nuclear weapon, preparing to save their asses. This conversation was not in the cards. The Marines at Con Thien were complaining they did not have enough claymores, and what they did have were not in the right places. A month prior to the attack, I put the mines where the commanders wanted them. I had no authority to deviate. Now commanders were telling me I needed to go back up to

Con Thien and help refortify the perimeter and double up the mines.

Everyone was uptight, and they knew I had no knowledge of where any main thrust or attack would occur; only the North Vietnamese enemy soldiers knew that.

After a few days went by, things started to somewhat settle down. Most Marines had observed the hard work and dangerous efforts it took to refortify the perimeter.

After helping reset the Con Thien perimeter with mines, I was ordered back down to Dong Ha some eight to ten miles south (refer to map B, p. 24). Then a lieutenant in Dong Ha told me I was chosen to go out on a search-and-destroy mission. That night I went with a recon team trying to locate a cache of small arms reported to us earlier in the day by one of the local villagers. I was always honored to work with recon. They were tough kids and knew what they were doing. I felt a little more secure when these guys were around. We ended up going out a few miles from the base perimeter when we came across the cache exactly where it was supposed to be. I was carrying four grenades and a backpack of explosives. I was also armed with a Thompson submachine gun with eight .45-caliber, thirty-round box clips. This was a great weapon when near or in elephant grass. I was set to blow up the cache of enemy weapons when we came under small-arms automatic fire. I set the explosives, and we were clearing the area while returning fire. Dong Ha, being so close, lit up the area with illumination flares. Enemy grenades were now being tossed at us, landing twenty to thirty yards short. Being a baseball catcher all my life, I developed a great arm, throwing guys out, trying to steal second base. I had emptied four of my eight clips and needed to save some ammo, so I started throwing my grenades. I threw all four grenades while the two Marines near me were laying down cover fire. Both these guys ended up giving me two of their own grenades. I ended up throwing all four of their grenades far enough that the enemy fire stopped. We hightailed it and got the hell out of there and back to the base. It was a successful night, and none of us were hurt. We blew up the enemy cache of weapons, and the mission was successful.

That night I acquired a reputation of being able to throw a grenade halfway to Hanoi. The recon guys felt really good about this, and I thought it was a good thing. After some thought, I realized everyone was going to want to utilize my throwing arm. I ended the night thinking this was not good, and it seemed my baseball skills could somehow get me killed. I fell asleep that night fearing my new conundrum.

Michael holding the Thompson submachine gun he carried on the mission to destroy a cache of weapons later that night.

(Picture courtesy of Michael Chapanar.)

Michael, the morning after successfully destroying a cache of enemy weapons and now with his mess gear, going to breakfast.

The hat he is wearing is inside out and upside-down just like his life at the time.

(Picture courtesy of Michael Chapanar.)

Michael assigned to outside-perimeter duty later that day.

(Picture courtesy of Michael Chapanar.)

CHAPTER 19

Six Teams

I was in my early teens when every summer I was playing for up to six different baseball teams. I was the catcher on all six teams. One team started and ended their season in the spring. One team was a summer-league team that played on weekdays. Another summer-league team played only night games. Our traveling team played on weekends during late summer and early fall. I also played on two all-star teams. Very seldom was there a conflicting schedule of games.

A different coach would drive over to our home and pick me up for games with that particular team. I was a pretty good catcher and really didn't care what team I was playing for. I just needed to play baseball and help that team win, never knowing it was preparation for the United States Marine Corps in so many ways.

While in Vietnam, I was assigned to every team you could imagine. I was a Marine who could blow up anything and also mine sweep for supply convoys as well as other combat operations. I repeatedly set up and put in mines. Very seldom with my own Eleventh Engineer Combat Battalion, I was continuously being assigned to go with any unit/ team that needed me that day or week like a roadrunner—here, there, and everywhere.

It was just like my old baseball days when at times I didn't realize or care in the moment what team I was on.

Most Marines I served with and everything I did in Vietnam became a blur overtime. I only cared about doing a good job and not getting anyone, including myself, killed.

The first nine months in Nam I was battle tested with infantry units, mechanized tank units, bridge engineering units, heavy-equipment units, and a few recon teams. I was being assigned anywhere needed.

It was the fog of war, and I was not concerned, nor did I care what team I was on. I was busy, and the clock kept moving; this was good.

Keeping track of who or what unit I was with and what events of the day took place was nonessential to me. I was not keeping a diary, and it never entered my mind to keep track of anything for future memoirs or a book. Dates, times, and places were all running together. I was concentrating on the task at hand in the moment and not anything else. Other Marines' names were of little consequence. I knew, if you became friends with anyone, you were only asking for a broken heart. First-name basis for the day was all you needed. In infantry training back at Camp Pendleton, the instructor told us to "look at the man to your right and look at the man to your left, within twelve months one or two of you will be dead." The message hit home and was proven true on the Vietnam DMZ in 1967. In Nam I made real friendships with no one; yet we were all like brothers.

Concentration was my only real friend. I had the innate ability to focus and concentrate after being a catcher on so many different baseball teams. I credit this quality with saving my life in the toughest situations in Vietnam. Concentration alone on the task at hand always kept me as calm as possible under the circumstances. Concentration was the reason for the other quality I had called situational awareness. Many so-called Marine friends had neither quality; it ended in death for them. There was one other thing you had to have to go along with these two qualities. It was called *luck*. I was also a man of belief and faith, and I prayed a lot. Yet I knew deep in my heart neither Jesus nor God was against these little Vietnamese people we were trying to kill in their own country. Most of the time when I prayed, I prayed for three things: concentration, situational awareness, and for friends and family back home.

On a late spring day, the Marines were taking a supply convoy to Khe Sanh. Route 9 was the road to Khe Sanh. Adjacent to Route 9 after passing Ca Lu ran a river a few hundred meters to the south along this dirt road. From the road it was downhill about one hundred meters to the river. North of Route 9 was a steep hill running up from the road. I traveled this road many times, and we had some serious problems doing so. On this day we had several tanks with 90-mm guns on them. There were also several Ontos vehicles in the convoy and many dump trucks full of supplies. I was hitching a ride on what we referred to as a 90-mm tank. I was sitting beside the turret, which had a somewhat oblong, rounded shape to it. Some Marines were riding in the back of the dump trucks, reading comic books. When I was called on, I would climb off the tank and mine sweep clearing sections of the dirt and muddy road. I was carrying a .45-caliber semiautomatic handgun and not a long gun because of minesweeping duties so there could be no dropping a cumbersome rifle on a mine and blowing yourself up. The Marine sitting next to me on the tank was carrying an M14 rifle. As we were slowly purring along, I noticed the Marine next to me kept falling asleep. It agitated me, and I kept waking him up. I was riding on the north side of the tank, looking up the hill when I spotted two VCs (Viet

Cong) about one hundred meters out with AK-47s in a mad dash from right to left in my view at the top of the hill. I immediately grabbed this Marine's rifle from his lap and began firing. The M14 had a selector on it for automatic firing similar to a machine gun. In a few seconds, the twenty-round clip was empty. I handed the rifle back to this stunned Marine and quickly climbed to the other side of the turret for cover. Just then what was later described to me as a 20-mm cannon was fired from across the river at our tank. It hit the south side of the turret and careened high off into the air. It was close enough, I felt the jolt and shock wave from the round sideswiping the tank. I only had my .45-caliber pistol, and we were being hit from both sides of the road with small-arms fire, heavy machine gunfire, and 20-mm cannon fire from across the river. All our tanks swung into action. The Ontos vehicle with its six recoilless rifles began firing, and the fight was on. The turret was turning on my tank, preparing to fire, and I was having a problem staying out of the way. After emptying my .45-caliber clip, I felt a Marine reach up, grab my boot, and yank me down off the tank. The bullets were zipping everywhere and clanging off the tank. I spotted a nearby downed, wounded Marine and picked up his M14. This M14 did not have an automatic selector on it and would only fire semiautomatic shots one at a time. I began taking dead aim one shot at a time at the flashes coming from across the river. The sound was totally deafening, and we were starting to receive incoming enemy artillery fire. One of our helicopter gunships finally arrived on scene and began firing rockets at targets across the river. It was a welcomed sight.

Within several minutes two planes had arrived, swooping in and dropping bombs.

The coordination of our counterattack was perfect. The explosions on the other side of the river were earth-shattering.

The Vietnamese gunfire was quieting down, and their artillery big guns were also being silenced.

A couple more choppers showed up a few minutes later, and our wounded or worse were taken away. I was never in the loop to find out the resulting casualties of the day. I did not know the names of anyone hurt or possibly killed. Like most cases, I was not familiar with many of the Marines on the convoy—maybe some familiar faces, but that was about it.

That night at Khe Sanh a captain wanted to speak to me. He found out I fired the first shots of the day. He was also told I swiped another Marine's rifle from his grasp to fire the first shots. The captain began yelling and screaming about taking another able-bodied

Marine's weapon from him and leaving the Marine defenseless in a critical situation. He said, "If it ever happens again, I would be held accountable with more than a verbal slap." Then he somewhat simmered down and said, "At least you weren't reading comic books or, worse yet, sleeping."

At the end of his sermon, he wanted to know if I thought I had shot and hit those two VC sons of bitches at the top of the hill. I said, "Captain, I have no idea!"

(Above) Michael preparing for minesweeping ahead of Ontos vehicles and convoy (yellow arrows pointing to three Ontos vehicles).

(Below) Michael is mine sweeping Route 9 to Khe Sanh.

(Pictures courtesy of Michael Chapanar.)

Every single time I awoke in Vietnam, I was scared; I was always concerned that today I would lose my nerve. It didn't matter what time you awoke, be it four thirty in the morning or two in the morning for guard duty on a perimeter, you awoke scared.

I could only keep my nerve by thinking of the other Marines I would be working with this day and for the next twelve to eighteen hours. Thinking ahead any further would garble my mind. I had no choice but to stay in the present. The thoughts of being killed or, worse yet, badly disfigured were constant, but you could never let yourself show other Marines your fear. Just the opposite, I would somehow muster up enough ego to look and act like I wasn't scared. Panicking in a situation was contagious, and you had to control yourself each and every hour.

When performing minesweeping activities, I was aware of everything bad that could happen. If you allowed yourself to go there, you could freeze up. Focusing on the sounds of your mine detector was paramount, and keeping your eyes clear by constantly blinking and refocusing your sight were something I did constantly. Every second while mine sweeping out ahead of the convoy, you were also aware you might be in someone's crosshairs. Each step could be your last if you stepped on the three prongs or tripped an almost-invisible trip wire. I desperately scanned the next step and ground I had to walk on. You persistently needed to trust in yourself and all your training. You also had to be aware of all the enemy tricks to wound or kill you. I was always asking questions of others who did what I was doing at every chance. We would forever discuss our experiences with one another, and it helped greatly. Seeing clearly every pebble, leaf, and stick or, better yet, seeing every ant or crawling bug on the ground were something I constantly had to do while not getting fixated on any one thing. I practiced this daily in secure areas as well. There were many times when I said to myself, *I can't do this anymore* and then quickly snapped out of it and regained my composure. I could never allow the people depending on me to see I was shaking in my boots. Then suddenly, I would raise my hand and wave off personnel. I found something or a cluster of various unknown devices.

The stress of the job, fear, or just the resulting traumatic heat of the day could result in loss of focus and death. A favorite trick used by the enemy was to cover a mine with fresh water-buffalo dung. Every disturbed piece of ground had to be checked again and again even if it was only hours before that you initially cleared the same area. Complacency and pure carelessness were a danger no matter how little time passed between each clearing.

The VC strategy was, they expected you to think the area was clean since your last sweep just hours before. Sometimes the enemy would dig many holes in the dirt road, only to fill in all but one with just dirt. The one they filled with an explosive device was the one the enemy was banking on. Not every mine or explosive device could be detected with a mine detector. So you would drop on your belly with a bayonet and a long, sharp-pointed rod with a ground-level view, probing the suspected area. Several times I was nose to nose with an active enemy mine, not knowing if it was a pressure activation device or an electronic enemy command detonation mine or both. If I ever came upon a command detonation device, fortunately for me, the guy on the other end was not in place at the time to detonate it.

My job was to locate enemy mines and somehow remove or destroy them. There were times when we pulled them out with a hook and long rope or just blew them up in place with our own ordinance. Sometimes with the right angle and tank we could shoot at it with a howitzer and blow it up in place.

Although putting in and setting mines were very stressful, it was much more so searching for them.

Battle Operations and Casualty Count from May 18, 1967, through July 14, 1967

Operation Hickory

From May 18, 1967, through May 28, 1967, *Operation Hickory* was mostly conducted in the compact area once again called Leatherneck Square around the firebase of Con Thien in Quang Tri Province (refer to map B, p. 24). I was very active in this search-and-destroy mission, blowing up several tunnels, bunkers, and loads of enemy weapons.

We lost 142 Marines killed in action with 896 Marines being wounded. The North Vietnamese Army and Viet Cong lost 789 killed in action.[6]

Operation Cimarron

Starting June 1, 1967, and lasting through July 2, 1967, *Operation Cimarron* was a land-clearing project from Con Thien to Gio Linh.[7] My job was loading up various perimeter areas with land mines while at the same time looking for and clearing enemy mines. North Vietnamese artillery, rockets, and sniper fire were our main concerns all through the period.

---

[6] Telfer, Major Gary L., Lieutenant Colonel Lane Rogers, USMC, and V.K. Fleming Jr. "The U.S. Marines in Vietnam: Fighting the North Vietnamese, 1967." Washington, D.C.: History and Museums Division, Headquarters, U.S. Marine Corps, 1984,p.30.

[7] Ibid, 161

Operation Buffalo

From July 2, 1967, to July 14, 1967, *Operation Buffalo* took place mostly in the southern half of the DMZ while also north of and around Con Thien. Enemy mortar fire and artillery were an hourly occurrence. *Resulting statistics were 159 Marines perished and 345 were wounded.* Enemy losses were again heavy at 1,290 dead.[8] It was a period in time I especially do not like to remember.

---

[8] Telfer, Major Gary L., Lieutenant Colonel Lane Rogers, USMC, and V.K. Fleming Jr. "The U.S. Marines in Vietnam: Fighting the North Vietnamese, 1967." Washington, D.C.: History and Museums Division, Headquarters, U.S. Marine Corps, 1984,p.104.

CHAPTER 20

Convoys to Khe Sanh

Once again on a convoy to Khe Sanh in the early summer of '67, we were attacked from both sides of Route 9. I was again riding on a tank with a 90-mm gun on it. We were close to the lead vehicles when all hell broke loose. Enemy gunfire was coming from what seemed like three hundred sixty degrees around us. On our left of Route 9, it was downhill to the river. On our right of Route 9 was the usual hillside leading up from the road. Less than a few hundred yards in front of us was a blind bend in the road. It was a perfect place for an ambush. We were surprise attacked and receiving machine gunfire from our left across the river. Mortar rounds were dropping in from the top of the hill and raining down on us. Small-arms fire was revving up from everywhere. The Ontos vehicles were positioning themselves to open fire. The shock waves from our 90-mm tanks firing would shake your eyeballs.

One of our lead vehicle trucks was hit in the grill with a shoulder-fired rocket from the bend, and it was ear-shattering. Within several minutes it was over. The smells of diesel fuel and gunpowder were strong. Now only the engines from our vehicles could be heard. Our jets were streaming over both sides of Route 9. On this day all I remember was how quickly it started and ended.

I was once again assigned to the supply convoy and not with my Eleventh Engineers. Like everything else, it was a blur. I was never told the results of these minutes of hell— rumors, yes, but none were the same. It was a twenty-vehicle convoy, and everyone had their own exaggerated version. Who the hell knew what happened, and how many enemies were attacking us? It could have been a dozen or many more. It was the fog of war. I kept firing my .45 at what I did not know. In the end, I was unscathed.

The attacks on our convoys were now becoming routine. We were getting hit almost every time we would run supplies on Route 9. Eventually, it became impassable, and Route 9 had to be closed. The bridges were constantly being blown, and we were sitting ducks. The minesweeping I was doing to keep the vehicles moving was nail-biting and dangerous. Finally, the Marine hierarchy shut the road down beyond Ca Lu to Khe Sanh, and they got no argument from me. Khe Sanh would now have to be resupplied by air only.

Michael on a convoy to Khe Sanh.

Top picture is blown bridge with an M50-A1 Ontos in place for security.

Lower picture is Michael setting up security around the bridge.

(Pictures courtesy of Michael Chapanar.)

CHAPTER 21

A Luau with the Ontos Pig

It was not until 2012 when I learned of the named combat operations I personally participated in. I was constantly yanked out of the Eleventh Engineer Battalion and embedded on missions with other units. Minesweeping assignments for supply convoys to Khe Sanh and Con Thien were endless, and we were always being attacked with artillery, rockets, and mortars.

The Ontos known as the Pig was one of our best tools on the DMZ, and with its six recoilless 106-mm rifles, it was deadly. The twenty-inch-wide tracks on this lightweight nine-ton vehicle would allow it to go in soft soil surrounding rice paddies and along muddy roads. It was highly mobile and fast. I knew most Ontos drivers and their crews on a first-name basis.

Potentially, it could fire one or all six 106-mm recoilless rifles at a time, shooting beehive rounds that sent out hundreds of darts per firing per barrel up to one quarter mile. These darts could stick enemy troops to surrounding trees, and it was known as the largest shotgun in the world. Several of the recoilless rifles had .50-caliber tracing round spotting guns attached that would fire first, making sure the recoilless rifle was on target prior to it firing. Each recoilless rifle could also fire a 106-mm armor-piercing round that was effective up to three thousand yards, and these were used as bunker busters.

In the summer of 1967, we were living underground at Ca Lu when four Pigs traveling Route 9 stopped on their way to Khe Sanh.

We conjured up an idea of digging out another underground living quarter, but this time we would put an Ontos in it. We put the Pig in the hole just deep enough so the recoilless rifles were aboveground. We then covered the vehicle with a tent, and you could not tell this beast was in the hole under the canvas tent. The Ontos was aimed at the most probable area an attack would occur. It could also do a three-hundred-sixty spin on a dime. The other Pigs went on to Khe Sanh. The backblast from firing the recoilless rifles could even kill anything within fifteen to twenty yards behind the vehicle. We had to make sure we were not behind it when it fired.

One night we heard voices and cans moving on the wire surrounding our perimeter, and without knowing when the Ontos was going to fire, it suddenly fired two of its rifles. No Marines aboveground were moving around at the time, and most of us were still underground playing cards and writing letters. When I heard the noise and surfaced, the Ontos fired two more shots. The backblast, fire, dirt, and debris were flying everywhere. A few seconds later it fired two more dart rounds. We sent up night illumination flares and observed more than a dozen enemies running down the hill and back down to the river area. A few minutes later hostile enemy artillery started pouring in on us. We heard our aircraft circling around, looking for artillery flashes. This quickly silenced their guns, and after several more minutes it all ended. Shortly after the event, most of us returned to our card games and letter writing underground. On this night none of us were hurt or injured. Thanks to the Ontos!

The Pig (Ontos) rolling along on
Route 9 in heavy bush.

(Pictures courtesy of Michael Chapanar.)

CHAPTER 22

Moving Civilians from the Blast Zone

We made every effort to elevate prestige of each village chief or hamlet elder. It was an endless task. It seemed we were always trying to move civilian Vietnamese around and out of harm's way. Making friends with people you didn't know what side they were on was difficult and dangerous. Winning the confidence of the population in the middle of a guerilla war was paramount. Yet when a member or members of a village were killed by either side, it would result in a loss of control and confidence of that village and the surrounding villages. We sometimes referred to them as the unfortunates of war. You could never fully trust any Vietnamese on the DMZ.

The pressure the villagers were under from Viet Cong tactics could make some villagers change sides overnight—today your friend, tomorrow your enemy, without changing clothes. The ongoing fight against the Viet Cong infrastructure in these villages and hamlets was referred to as the other war.

Every Marine's job was to befriend the civilian people at every opportunity given. You became so familiar with some of the Vietnamese children, your heart would ache for them. Then from that day on you might never see them again, not ever knowing their fate.

I became very close to one little ten-year-old boy; his name was Hun. He would always wear his American Cub Scout hat I had given him. I bought it for him on an ADM training trip back to Okinawa. His parents had been killed a few months before I met him. He would always be somewhere around the Dong Ha Combat Base. When I would have an assignment stringing wire on the perimeter of the base, I would anxiously wait for him to show up. He was such a cute and polite kid, always smiling and happy. I would save up my candy that was in our C-rat boxes and give it to Hun. If nowhere else, Hun could always be found somewhere near an entrance to the base. He was getting to the point of being able to speak some English. Hun was acquiring so much candy; it was like Halloween every day. Soon he had quite a few Vietnamese kids hanging around with him, and he was the leader of the pack. This went on for several months whenever I would go back to Dong Ha. I always looked forward to seeing him. I began to have thoughts of someday adopting him, but I had no knowledge of how this would work.

After not seeing him for several weeks, a few Marines began to notice his absence. We couldn't get any information of his whereabouts. Finally, he totally disappeared, never to be found or seen by anyone again. We were left to surmise the Viet Cong did not accept him being so friendly with the Marines, and he became another unfortunate of war!

(Top picture) Michael involved in civil work helping to move civilians away from the DMZ.

(Bottom picture) Michael with his little Vietnamese friend Hun.

(Pictures courtesy of Michael Chapanar.)

Battle Operations and Casualty Count from July 14, 1967, through February 28, 1969

Operation Hickory II

Operation Hickory II commenced on July 14, 1967, and lasted only two days. The mission was to destroy enemy fortifications, mortar, and artillery positions. The operation took place from the southern edge of the DMZ down to the Cam Lo, Bo Dieu, and Cua Viet rivers. *Cumulative friendly casualties were 4 killed and 99 wounded.*[9]

Operation Kingfisher

Operation Kingfisher was prosecuted from July 16, 1967, to October 31, 1967, again in Leatherneck Square, and the objective was to block the North Vietnamese Army from entering the eastern Quang Tri Province. I

---

[9] Operation Hickory II–Amtrac.org

was sent back to Okinawa for the third time from July 22 through the end of July for continuous training with a nuclear bomb and returning to Vietnam approximately the first week of August. This trip turned out to be my third and final training trip to Okinawa. Although my part in Operation Kingfisher did last through October 1967, the first week in September I became a barber cutting hair and was left out of the September and October field combat operations. I was now just sitting in Dong Ha as a barber cutting hair and waiting to be activated and deployed with a nuclear weapon. We were receiving heavy artillery weekly, and Dong Ha played a big role in Operation Kingfisher.

On September 3 while near my barbershop, rockets hit our ammo-and-fuel dump, which blew everything sky-high. It was the largest fireworks show I ever witnessed in my life. Every Fourth of July thereafter reminds me of September 3, 1967.

In the end, Operation Kingfisher resulted in the death of 340 Marines with over 1,461 Marines wounded while 1,117 North Vietnamese Army troops and Viet Cong were killed.[10]

Operation Kentucky

Operation Kentucky started on November 1, 1967, and continued through February 28, 1969. It was another operation in an effort to secure the Con Thien, Cam Lo, and Dong Ha combat bases. I was only involved in this operation for three weeks until November 22, 1967, when my tour of duty in Vietnam ended. The month of November 1967 was an extremely busy month of rehearsals and drills of which, I believe, included an actual partial deployment with a probable authentic

---

[10] Historycentral.com/Vietnam/kingfisher.html

tactical nuclear weapon. *Operation Kentucky snuffed out the lives of 520 U.S. Marines while wounding 2,698.* The Operation killed 3,839 of the enemy in a very small area of South Vietnam.[11]

If you know of anyone killed in Vietnam, simply type in your browser "www.virtual-wall.org" and select the first letter of their last name. Scroll through the list of U.S. personnel killed. I'm sure everyone knows of someone listed on the wall.

---

[11] Telfer, Major Gary L., Lieutenant Colonel Lane Rogers, USMC, and V.K. Fleming Jr. "The U.S. Marines in Vietnam: Fighting the North Vietnamese, 1967." Washington, D.C.: History and Museums Division, Headquarters, U.S. Marine Corps, 1984,p.74. Also, Wikipedia.org operation kentucky

CHAPTER 23

John Vann's Visit to Dong Ha

One day late in the summer of '67, my assignments for the day were cancelled. I was told to stay close to the company battalion tent area. This was not unusual because of constant unexpected nuclear weapon deployment drills. I was hanging out when I heard an unmistakable Southern-tone voice say, "Hey, Marine, how ya doin'?" It was John Paul Vann. We had not seen each other for several years, so we had a lot of catching up to do. I didn't know at the time the magnitude of the role he was playing in the grand scheme of things in Vietnam. He said he was in the Dong Ha area doing some intel gathering and needed to talk with several people, and he could not pass up an opportunity to visit. It was good to see a familiar face and a family member here of all places.

We reminisced about the family and brought each other up-to-date on news from home. He asked about my fiancée, Angela. I realized he had been keeping up with the family. How else would he know about Angela? I corrected him, though, because Angela and I were not engaged yet. John had asked if I had taken any R & R. When I said, "No, not yet," he answered, "I know you haven't."

I was baffled on just how he knew I had not taken R & R (rest and relaxation away from Vietnam). As it turned out, I never did take any real R & R. We went to the mess hall to eat, and we finished up our visit.

There was no mention of any nuclear weapon activities, and I was not about to bring up the subject. John didn't say who else he needed to talk to on the DMZ, but he did say he had a few other things to do, and then he had to get back. He mentioned he heard a lot of good things through the family grape-vine. This got us talking about him and me and our grape-picking days in my aunt Mary's backyard. I would always take a bat, glove, and some baseballs to my aunt Mary's. We reminisced about him hitting ground balls in her backyard and playing ping-pong in the basement. It was a fun and sorely needed chat. Then he had a very serious look on his face and said, "Mike, I know you have been employed doing some important and serious work. If you are called upon, I know you will answer the call." Without hesitation, I replied, "Yes, John, I will." I felt right then and there he was aware of my situation, and it might have been one of the reasons he came to visit. I think he needed to be confident I would carry out the assignment, and he wanted to say goodbye. He made a statement in the form of a question that verified my thoughts. "Mike," he said, "most civilians have been cleared from certain areas on the DMZ. You know that, right?" I answered, "Yes, I know." In the end, we shook hands, and we hugged. I was feeling a lump in my throat as we said our goodbyes. I was also feeling, one or both of us might never get back to my aunt Mary's and enjoy picking grapes and hitting grounders together again. It was the last time I ever saw John Paul Vann.

CHAPTER 24

Career Advisory Interview

Sunday, August 20, 1967, I was back in Dong Ha for a day of rest when I was summoned to the headquarters battalion tent. The sergeant told me he wanted to go over some future planning and paperwork. He laid a Career Advisory Interview Guide and Checklist (Form 1133) on his desk. I was looking at the form when he informed me we needed to discuss my future military career. As I rolled my eyes, I said, "You've got to be serious!" He actually wanted to talk about extending my tour of duty in Vietnam for another six months, promotional opportunities, and reenlistment options. He started out talking about an officer's program upon return to the United States and a possible promotion to warrant officer. I thought this guy lost his mind and that he was joking. As I told him so, he jumped up and said, "No, Lance Corporal, it's not a joke." He said he was authorized to make me some offers. If I were to extend my stay in Nam for another six months, in the end there would be a large salary increase and a crossover promotion to officer in the future.

At the beginning of his presentation, I did not believe him. Thirty minutes into the presentation, I knew he was serious. I was trying to digest his words while not saying a word myself. He then stared me in the eyes and said, "Well, what do you think?" I stared him back in his eyes and said, "I don't care if they make me general, I'm out of here in ninety-four days, my friend!" The sergeant seemed flabbergasted I could turn such an offer down. He had no idea I was currently involved in a probable suicide assignment. Did this guy want me to extend my stay until I was dead or what? No, thanks. As he finished the presentation, I watched him write on his form: "This man has no desire to make service a career." I stood up and said, "You got that right, pal," and I immediately left his tent.

I still have a dated copy of the form and his remarks in my possession.

CHAPTER 25

Cut the Sides Close

In September of 1967 I was told, combat, as I knew it, was over for me. I was now back in Dong Ha—no more sweeping for mines, no more taking out or putting in U.S. mines, no more running supply convoys, and no more guard duty, stringing wire, or setting explosives.

I was told I was now a barber and given instructions not to leave my living quarters (tent area) unless I was going to the mess hall approximately one hundred twenty yards away. They had constructed a barber chair and a 10'×10' barbershop. I was also instructed to cut everyone's hair who wanted a haircut.

I acquired a hand-squeezed set of clippers, a comb, and a pair of scissors and was able to find a piece of polished metal to use as a decent-size mirror. In the beginning it seemed the clippers pulled more hair out than it cut. There were very few repeat customers at first. A few days passed, and I finally did get the hang of it.

I spent hours sitting in that barber chair, reading the same old *Playboy* magazines over and over, waiting for the next customer or enemy artillery round. Then a group of guys would come in, and I squeezed those clippers until I thought my hand and forearm would fall off. A few Marines were picky, but my main concern was trying not to draw blood. Some guys had moles or scabs, and some guys were just crusty and stank. It was no hair on the sides and short on the top. If they were going back to the United States soon, I would cut them some slack.

I had to take a little more time with the brass. Now I was getting confident and would even trim their mustaches.

Everyone wanted to know how I pulled this gig. Kiddingly, I told them I was a barber in civilian life. They knew I was not a barber. Some offered me a coin or two, but I had orders not to accept money.

It seemed as if there were rumors leaking out about me having something to do with nukes. All the guys were starting to be a little friendlier toward me, or maybe it was just my imagination working overtime. The various drills and rehearsals I went through were sometimes visible at the airstrip at night. Marines were starting to figure things out. These exercises were hard to hide 100 percent of the time. My commander would bark out orders, which could possibly be heard by the guys operating our refrigerated body-bag trucks or the mechanics who were taking care of aircraft.

From the time I arrived in December 1966 to September 1967, the faces in our platoon, company, and battalion had changed because of all the reasons of war. I was told Willard had been shot and was aboard a hospital ship. I also heard Gem was wounded and sent back to the United States.

There were a lot of fresh faces who had no reason to dislike me. Maybe they even had reasons to love me. Guys were bringing me goodies back from the mess hall and acted as if they knew something.

No one would bring up the subject of nukes, and I couldn't talk about it if they did. The only war I was dealing with now were rockets and heavy artillery strikes. Dong Ha was being hit several times a week, sometimes day after day.

Dong Ha was always receiving artillery, and there was no way to get away from the shelling. The first week in September 1967 enemy rockets directly hit our main ammo-and-fuel dump. It was a horrific day, hard to watch and listen to.

I had a foxhole two feet from my barber chair. It seemed I was in that hole all the time. Keeping it clean, dry, and free of rodents was an endless job, but it was the best foxhole on the DMZ.

One day a dud artillery round hit some twenty yards away from the shop. I looked, but my name was not on it.

Until I was summoned to do a tactical nuclear weapon drill, the cutting-hair gig was good.

Michael took this photo just prior to jumping
into his barbershop foxhole for cover.

Two small rockets hit first then the
third rocket hit the ammo dump.

September 3, 1967.

Explosions from ammo dump
continued for hours.

The ammo-dump blast sounded
like an atomic bomb.

This scene was at the beginning of the attack;
I only had seconds to take this picture.

(Picture courtesy of Michael Chapanar.)

Michael guarding his barbershop.

Michael retrieved dud artillery round
that landed twenty yards away.

(Pictures courtesy of Michael Chapanar.)

CHAPTER 26

Seared into My Mind

While sitting in my barber chair, I was thinking back to the last training trip in July. The July trip to Okinawa turned out to be my final one. Every trip was more intense than the one before as they added something new each time. It was explained to me and seared into my mind that, logically, if we used a tactical nuclear weapon, it would be proactive or preempted on our terms and conditions.

Waiting to counterattack with a tactical nuke would be reactive and could possibly take away many options and meteorological advantages. It stood to reason, the option to use a nuke while the masses had gathered or were gathering was logical and not after they dispersed around the countryside, especially deep into the southern half of South Vietnam.

How could you light up a nuke when you were fighting your enemy belt to belt and tossing grenades? How was it possible to use a nuke at close range? Also, not knowing what other conditions might exist and what the blast patterns would be when the enemy was attacking could be a large problem.

For these reasons, I was told the target would be in a favorable geographical terrain with the right atmospheric conditions and on our terms. We could also radiate an entire area as a blocking force and limit their infiltration routes as well as destroying the masses at one time. It all made sense to me though I was not the nuclear war planner.

The CIA drilled into my head that a tac-nuke mission might not only save a base, but also the entire war. I was told repeatedly there was a strong chance it could bring an end to the war, thereby saving millions of additional lives from the war's collateral damage on both sides. This was a good thing and was definitely a motivating factor to carry out the operation. I never imagined not doing my duty when called upon. I didn't want to see more people die than what it would take to stop the madness and killing. Every life was precious, even the lives of the enemy.

Getting to the target as quickly as possible could not be understated. Minutes and seconds could be the deciding factors for a successful outcome. The window of opportunity to use a nuke would be very small. Being totally prepared and ready to deploy at a moment's notice was paramount. Timing, speed, and proficiency would make or break the mission. I was taught there would be no time for thinking, only reacting with fierce concentration and relying on trained habits.

If any of this ever made sense, it was in the fall of 1967. The DMZ was quickly becoming the right time and the right place.

CHAPTER 27

A Rehearsal with Three Friends

One afternoon I was summoned to the airstrip and quickly found it to be a practice drill/rehearsal. I hadn't done a drill for a couple of weeks, and going this long without a drill in the late summer and early fall of 1967 was unusual.

The handler in charge of this operation seemed calm. He said we were going to stage a drill in a secure area. The drill was going to be set in the corner of a rice paddy and would take several hours to complete. He actually grinned when he told me I would be working with three friends today. I knew from rehearsals in Okinawa the three friends were a couple of dead rats and a dead snake. We went out to the location by helicopter although we stayed within several miles of Dong Ha. Two fresh-cut bushes with cement can tie-down anchors were placed in the corner of the rice paddy near the high-ground walkway and canal. This gave me the ability to move the bushes around for cover if needed. It was my job to put the rats and snake in place on the walk-way as a deterrent and barrier. Some type of odorless repellent was sprayed on the rats and snake to keep other rodents and birds away.

I was wearing a wetsuit under my cam-ouflaged utilities with goggles and a snorkel for submerging if necessary.

All geared up with the normal harnesses, I was thinking the bomb and all the gear felt exceptionally heavy; maybe the bomb case and package were filled with rocks today.

The mission that day was to enter into the corner of the rice paddy in about eighteen inches of water while keeping the camouflaged bomb package from submerging and dry. I was partially submerged, keeping the bomb container above water against the canal bank. I held on to the dummy bomb and the anchored bushes to stay submerged. I was only carrying my .45-caliber pistol. The dead rodents were in place, and I was now secured and hidden away in the paddy. The CIA handler in charge of the operation said they would be back in a few hours. "Stay here, don't move, and we don't want to see you until we return. We will be watching at all times." With no radio or signaling devices, I was set to stay out of sight for several hours. Five hours later it was getting dark. Night illumination flares were being shot up every few minutes from Dong Ha. Finally, the handler and the chopper returned. We rounded up the gear and headed back to the base. My fingers were shriveled up, and I was shivering cold. Back in the tent at the airstrip, I got out of the wetsuit and changed into dry clothing. After going over the day's mission and a debriefing, my commander said a steak and hot mashed potatoes were waiting at the mess hall. At that point I was all in. The day's work was over. The cold-water challenge and testing my resolve were a success. He knew it, and he knew I knew it.

Whatever I was fearful of that day, I was not about to tell him. Whenever I was nervous or claustrophobic, I concentrated on two things—Angela and the third brick down in her fireplace. I concentrated on the third brick down a lot.

I was told in Okinawa, water would most likely be involved in the Vietnam mission. I had a fifty-five-gallon drum filled with water behind the barbershop.

Some Marines thought it was for washing their clothes, but I had an old washing machine with a handwringer on the side of the shop for washing clothes. As many as six times a week, I would jump into the fifty-five-gallon drum full of water and stay in it longer and longer each time. It was self-survival training. It was crazy, but I had a tremendous desire to survive. It was also working, and I could stay in the cold drum of water longer and longer each day. One day while in the drum, I visualized watching the James Bond movie *Goldfinger*. In the movie Mr. Auric Goldfinger, the villain, called his operation to use an atomic bomb Operation Grand Slam. I thought this ironic as the name *grand slam* was a baseball term. The villain, Mr. Goldfinger, perhaps enjoyed baseball too.

I had two five-gallon fuel cans filled with water and tied together behind the shop. I then built a sloped ramp, using sandbags and a couple of eight-foot-long, two-by-twelve planks. I would grab the cans, walk up the ramp, and do squats at the top. This kept my legs, core, and shoulders in shape. It also helped with balance. The weight totaled about ninety pounds. Going forward up the ramp and doing ten squats at the top one leg at a time, then backing down off the ramp made for a good workout especially after several sets. It was perfect! I essentially had my own gym and spa area. When someone came into the shop for a haircut, I would jump out of the drum of water while still in my skivvies and/or drop the cans and start cutting hair. Looking wet and cold was not unusual during the monsoon season, and nobody really noticed or cared what I was doing behind my barbershop.

Michael holding one of the two cans he used
for squatting exercises behind his barbershop.

The name of the Marine next to him,
who needed a haircut, is unknown.

(Picture courtesy of Michael Chapanar.)

CHAPTER 28

The Media and Museum

Business Insider

The online site Business Insider, in February 2014, published an article titled, "The 9 Most Interesting Details Behind America's Backpack Nukes" by Jeremy Bender.[12] The following excerpts from his article are paraphrased, and the entire article may be found online:

> At the height of the Cold
> War in Europe, the United

---

[12] Jeremy Bender, "9 Facts about the US's Backpack Nukes," *Business Insider*, February 3, 2014, https://www.businessinsider.com/9-facts-about-the-uss-backpack-nukes-2014-2.

States was seriously considering the use of backpack sized nuclear weapons for tactical strikes. He went on to explain that D. B. Grady and Adam Rawnsley, writing for *Foreign Policy*, went through a treasure trove of recently declassified information and revealed the pure insanity of backpack nukes.

The idea was not to lead to an all-out nuclear apocalypse. The "small" weapons, still more powerful than Hiroshima in most cases, were embraced for tactical purposes. These weapons would obliterate a battlefield and irradiate much of the surrounding area. The B-54 Atomic Demolition Munition entered the U.S. arsenal in 1964.

Elite soldiers from the Army, Navy, and Marines were trained to use these nukes in a variety of battlefields. The use of these weapons on battlefronts stretched from Eastern Europe all the way over to Korea. Backpack nukes were meant to be part of the US military's effort to ensure the containment of communist forces. No weapon was more ridiculous than the rollout of atomic demolition munitions (ADMs) in 1954. These nukes had the goal of creating impassible irradiated landscapes and craters that would bottleneck enemy soldiers. In case of enemy advancement the ADMs could be set off to destroy the enemy forces. In case of being captured by enemy forces, the ADM teams carried with them enough conventional explosives to destroy the nuclear weapon. This explosion would scatter nuclear waste, but would not result in a nuclear detonation. Instructors would insist an ADM person or team had to stay within visual range of the detonation to ensure success. All devices relied on mechanical timers for their detonators, which were inherently unreliable. These timers could vary by going off as much as eight minutes early or 13 minutes late. To pull off a successful mission a team would have to infiltrate enemy positions, sneak up on them while carrying an unwieldy nuclear weapon, set it, and wait for it to explode.

The same Adam Rawnsley, along with David Brown, published an article for *stuff. co.nz* in April of 2014. They wrote the following of which I have taken additional excerpts:

> To receive ADM qualifications, soldiers had to be screened through the Defense Department's per-

sonnel reliability program to make sure they were trustworthy and mentally stable. The soldiers with the best records and most experience could end up on the ADM team. It is mandatory a team divide the code that unlocks the cover plate. To protect the bomb from unauthorized use, the ADM's control panel was sealed by a cover plate secured by a combination lock. In addition, the two-man rule, dictates that no individual service member has the ability to arm a nuclear weapon. A glow-in-the-dark paint was applied to the lock allowing a person to unlock the bomb at night. If the person or team was lucky enough to be alive after the weapon detonated, with the odds stacked heavily against survival, they could then rely on their wits and escape the area. Traveling through enemy air space to their destination, operating covertly behind enemy lines, then sneaking up on hostile forces with a hand carried nuclear weapon and waiting uncomfortably close before the bomb exploded—the mission would be nothing short of preposterous. They were all said to be volunteer missions.[13]

* * *

I carried the B-54 atomic demolition munition in front of me, harnessed to my shoulders and above my belt. It stood approximately eighteen inches tall and was encased in an aluminum and fiberglass frame. It rounded to a bullet shape on one end and had a twelve-inch-diameter control panel on the other. The bomb's total weight, depending on the type of outside packaging, could be as much as ninety pounds. The weapon's *minimum* explosive yield was one kiloton, equivalent to one thousand tons of TNT. The ADM B-54 bomb had more than one yield setting.

---

[13] Adam Rawnsley and David Brown, "When Elite Troops Strapped Nukes to their Backs," Stuff, April 2, 2014, http://www.stuff.co.nz/world/europe/9682966/When-elite-troops-strapped-nukes-to-their-backs.

What was once a top-secret nuclear weapon is now a tourist attraction. Today, visitors to the U.S. government's National Museum of Nuclear Science and History in Albuquerque, New Mexico, can get their picture taken with the weapon.

(Picture obtained from the National Museum of Nuclear Science and History, Albuquerque, New Mexico.)

The picture above is a fully assembled bomb and its case on display at the National Museum of Nuclear Science and History in Albuquerque, New Mexico. This is a similar bomb that was once top secret during the Vietnam War.

The picture below is a partially dismantled ADM. I witnessed the bomb in this stage on several occasions in training although I was never tasked with dismantling the bomb to this degree other than for training purposes and the knowledge. The purpose of this picture is to show some of the intricate pieces that make up a nuclear bomb.

(Department of Defense picture.)

(Picture obtained from "Declassified U.S. Nuclear Test Film #31," YouTube.)

The picture above is for illustrative purposes only and is *not* me. I never experienced jumping out of an aircraft with a bomb package. This weapon was nicknamed a *backpack nuke* and could be carried on your back with the right package and straps. I was tasked with carrying the weapon in front of me and never carried it on my back. Although I transported the weapon strapped on similar to what is pictured, the harness configuration and straps I used were different and not designed for parachuting.

1967 CBS News Special Report

Mike Wallace of CBS, along with Robert Schakne and John Laurence, anchored a special news report that aired on a Sunday, October 1, 1967, on national television. The report illustrated visuals, timelines, geographical layouts, and a sense of what both sides were thinking. In the report, *John Laurence* clearly stated the Marines were talking about the need for *tactical nuclear weapons!*

The report may be viewed online by entering, "The Ordeal of Con Thien."[14]

---

[14] "The Ordeal of Con Thien," http:/www.c-span.org/video/?305185-1/the-ordeal-con-thien.

The following are excerpts from the *historical* CBS report:

General William Westmoreland—Commander of United States Forces

"Precisely, their objective is political and psychological and is designed to weaken the will of the American people to make it appear in American and world opinion that they are stronger than they are in fact and to discourage our resolve."

Lt. General R. E. Cushman Jr.

General Cushman was the commanding general of the Third Marine Division. He was the general who personally signed my nuclear weapons orders and was interviewed in this special report, stating the following:

"Well, when you sit in a place such as that and night comes on, you really have to rely upon yourself and upon supporting fires, and naturally, the confidence may not be as great as it is back here where I can see the many forces that can be brought to bear and which those right on the spot may not be aware."

Robert Schakne—CBS Reporter

"There's not likely to be much change as long as the monsoons last. The heavy rains are supposed to start this month and last two or three months, and during this period it is unlikely the Marines can reopen the roads. Now, whether the North Vietnamese are going to use this period to continue to shell the Marines or whether they will try something more substantial is, of course, something that nobody on this side can answer. But during the monsoons Con Thien is most isolated, airpower is most limited, and the Marines will be most vulnerable."

John Laurence—CBS Reporter

"The military can no longer justify this war with a casualty count. It may be that more Marines are dying along the DMZ than enemy. What seems to be overlooked is the ability of the North Vietnamese to escalate this war step-by-step with Washington. You begin to suspect that we've reached the limits of our present strategy when the generals are talking openly about an invasion of the north, and the men around Con Thien are talking about the need for *tactical nuclear weapons!*

Mike Wallace—CBS Anchor

"Lyndon Johnson understands, a defeat or withdrawal now at Con Thien would be, for him, a political Dien Bien Phu. The president's dilemma is how to persuade the North Vietnamese to quit up there. The fall monsoons have just begun, and they will go on until February, hampering American airpower, depriving the men on the ground of at least some of the air support they desperately need."

* * *

This report aired on TV sets across America! My mother and Angela watched the program live. They understood I was in the DMZ area. Mother wrote and said the CBS report talked about the possible use of tactical nuclear weapons. *I quickly burned the letter.*

* * *

CBS and Walter Cronkite

Walter Cronkite was truly an unbiased news anchor. The CBS newsman was known to be the most trustworthy voice on television news without editorializing.

Cronkite became disturbed with images of the Vietnam War he was reporting. Shortly after the Tet Offensive, he decided he had to go see for himself. Upon return from Vietnam, Walter Cronkite gave an editorial report. It was such a personal departure from his character that the nation was shocked when on February 27, 1968, he stated, "The war could not be won, and we are mired in a stalemate." This was also remarkable because of the fairness doctrine, a federal policy requiring broadcasters to remain neutral about the great questions of the day. The doctrine was rescinded in 1987.

Cronkite's analysis was right—we were not winning, nor would we. President Johnson knew Cronkite's opinion given to millions of viewers meant the end of his presidency. The iconic news reporter had witnessed for himself that Westmoreland and Johnson were, in fact, not telling the truth.

On February 27, 1968, Walter Cronkite became a big part of the war.

RAND

RAND, acronym for "research and development," is known as a think tank of professionals and the government's most prominent contractor. The RAND institution helps improve research and analysis, providing effective solutions that address the challenges facing the public and private sectors around the world. While RAND is not the media, in 2010 they published a book entitled *RAND in Southeast Asia.* On Page 292 of their 671-page book, I have borrowed three sentences that I have known to be true for over fifty years:

1. The Offensive actually began in November of 1967, when the communist staged a series of attacks in remote areas to draw South Vietnamese and U.S. Forces from their cities.

2. In late 1967, reports indicated that North Vietnamese had amassed a force of 40,000 men, consisting of four infantry divisions reinforced by two artillery regiments and armored units, near Khe Sanh.

3. Westmoreland moved 6,000 U.S. Marines to the area. His plan of a counterattack included massive bombing and the potential use of *Tactical Nuclear Weapons.*[15]

The New York Times

On October 6, 2018, the *New York Times* (Asia Pacific) printed a story, "U.S. General Considered Nuclear Response in Vietnam War, Cable Shows" by David E. Sanger. A version of this article appeared in print on page A1 of the New York edition with the

---

[15] Duong Van Mai Elliott, "RAND in Southeast Asia," *RAND*, 2010, p. 292.

headline, "U.S. Commander Moved to Place Nuclear Arms in South Vietnam."[16]

The *New York Times* reported on recently uncovered declassified top secret documents regarding *Operation Fracture Jaw*. It told of the planning and setting into place a possible *counterattack* with a nuclear weapon around the DMZ area and how the plan was shut down. The article clearly exposes General Westmoreland's thoughts in January and February of 1968. What this article did not uncover or talk about were the previous months in the fall of 1967.

In the fall of 1967, the general was just as willing to use the weapon to *prevent* an enemy overrun attack and avoid a repeat of the Dien Bien Phu attack that took place on the French in 1954. General Westmoreland's idea in the fall months of 1967 was to use a

---

[16] David E. Sanger, "U.S. General Considered Nuclear Response in Vietnam War, Cable Shows," *New York Times, Asia Pacific*, October 6, 2018.

tactical nuclear weapon on a first strike and not just as a counterattack measure. This would clearly send a message to Hanoi.

Con Thien was a major concern, but the Khe Sanh Combat Base near the DMZ was keeping Westmoreland from getting a good night's sleep. There was no conceivable way President Johnson or General Westmoreland were going to allow the slaughter of six thousand U.S. Marines and other military personnel to happen at Khe Sanh or Con Thien in the fall of '67, let alone become the first American commanders in history to be humiliated and disgraced by losing a war.

Perhaps, the initial planning stages of *Operation Fracture Jaw* started in October 1966. In August of '67 I was a hardened combat Marine fully trained, waiting for the final order to carry the bomb to its ultimate destination.

The *New York Times*, perhaps, missed the better story.

CHAPTER 29

The Battleground Model and Mission

The brass and hierarchy, including President Johnson, were so concerned that, eventually, a model of the entire Khe Sanh area was also kept in the White House. Westmoreland thought Khe Sanh was going to be the decisive and main event.

I had witnessed the same type of models of both Khe Sanh and Con Thien in Okinawa in July of 1967, complete with hills, mountains, valleys, jungles, roads, rivers, and bridges and also flags and pins representing enemy divisions, battalions, and units. It was all very convincing that we had it right. They had me convinced, the only way to make sure we did not lose one or both of our fire-bases during the coming monsoon season was to use a tactical nuclear weapon that would destroy them dead in their tracks. I was told, in no uncertain terms, the repercussions of such use of force were not my concern and way above my paygrade.

I was now a short-timer with little time left to serve in Vietnam. In the back of my mind I was thinking maybe the all-out ground attack on Khe Sanh or Con Thien might not happen on my watch. It was the only glimmering light I saw at the end of the tunnel. Mostly, I heard a loud train coming, and there was no slowing down. Every day left in Vietnam fortified the idea, an attack was more imminent than the day before and certain to happen.

It was a race against time, and I had no control of anything. In the middle of the night I would be awakened and taken to the airstrip, not knowing if this time was real or just another drill. I was so used to these procedures they would have to ramp up the next one even more to keep me believing this one might be the real deal.

I witnessed quite a few Marines lose their lives with just weeks left to serve in Nam. I was ready to die, but not within weeks or days of going home. Every day the guys would come back to Dong Ha, saying something big was going to happen soon.

I knew the Marine Corps or CIA cancelled my last training trip back to Okinawa scheduled in September for a good reason. They cancelled it to keep me close at hand and safe with their thumb and eyes on me, knowing exactly where I was 24-7, ready to deploy. The Marine Corps had too much time and effort invested to lose me now. I was also thinking I might be the only one who made it through the entire process thus far.

The barbershop was a treasure trove of information. I would ask everyone coming in from the field, what was the latest going on. Most Marines were willing to talk about their previous weeks' activity north of Route 9 and just south of the DMZ. I was familiar with the entire area (also referred to as the dead Marine zone). Very few Marines had clearance to know of the intelligence I had learned during my last trip to Okinawa.

At this point the streaming information I was getting from the Marines sitting in my barbershop chair were clearly validating those intelligence reports. Enemy movement, contacts, and activity were on the rise.

I was now more concerned than ever although I couldn't tell a soul. I needed to act as if I didn't know a thing. I also had to act calm and relaxed when Marines would kid me about how I got such a cushy barbershop gig. Little did they know I had been dreaming of that smelly, dirty, homeless garbageman job I had before joining the Marine Corps. The refuse job had no mental stress and was not going to get me killed.

Lieutenants were the first to come in and get cleaned up with a haircut upon returning to Dong Ha from other firebases on the DMZ. The lieutenants needed to set an example and clean up first. They were also a good source of current information and were the most willing to talk about their men and missions. It was as if they wanted to share everything. I was acting like a barber, but felt more like a psychiatrist or a priest. Their stories were so detailed and sad. Some broke down and cried, and the more I consoled them, the more they told me.

It was all adding up. Something extreme was happening around us, and something large was going to take place very soon—

something more than the normal rockets and artillery screaming in on us here at Dong Ha.

Everyone sensed the enemy buildup was a lot more than what met the eye.

The weather had turned bad, and we were in the midst of the monsoon rainy season. Bad weather days, when air support was all but nonexistent, brought upon us the most deafening and ground-shaking artillery attacks coming from what seemed to be all directions. You had better be close to a hole and not on your way to the mess hall. Just a few months before, on September 3, a rocket hit our ammo dump here in Dong Ha, and it felt like an earthquake. The explosions coming from our ammo-and-fuel dump lasted for hours. Trying to run in the mud was like trying to run in the ocean neck-deep in water. Our boots were always heavy with mud, and you could easily lose a boot in the suction if not strapped on tightly.

The guys coming in for a haircut constantly stomped their feet and shook the mud off their boots inside my 10'×10' shop before jumping into the barber chair. They would laugh and joke, insisting I had nothing else to do, but clean up the place with the shovel sitting in the corner. Some Marines resented my barbershop assignment. They would ask, "Have you dodged any bullets today?" Most Marines were not in a good mood and just wanted to go home themselves, but they would also notice the shop was ventilated with shrapnel holes and would laugh even more. I retrieved a dud round that landed pretty close a week earlier. I had it propped up near the entrance of the shop until one day a lieutenant colonel came in for a haircut and told me to get rid of that thing out there.

On this particular day it was partly cloudy with no rain and a fairly high cloud ceiling.

Choppers were actively moving Marines around from firebase to firebase.

The constant roar of our fighter jets could be heard in the background, and supply planes were constantly landing and departing our airstrip here in Dong Ha.

The day was shaping up to be an uneventful day with weather being so cooperative. The enemy would generally lay low on days like this. Their MO was to move around at night or in times of bad weather.

I knew the mess hall would be busy today. I also figured I would be cutting a lot of hair today. At breakfast I smuggled a half-dozen, rare, fresh eggs from the kitchen at the mess hall. All I needed were heat and water, and I would have the luxury of soft-boiled eggs all day and never have to leave the shop. I would pass on the fresh, hot boll weevil bread. The dough used to make the bread at the mess hall always had dead boll weevils in it. Some

Marines were forever betting one another on how many weevils were in each roll. Most didn't care.

That afternoon there was a slight breeze blowing to the north. I felt something odd and had a premonition. That night I had a bad feeling as I wrote letters to my mother and Angela and fell asleep after writing, never bothering to take off my boots. At 1:00 a.m. I was quietly awoken and taken by jeep to the airstrip.

Few people were there when my CIA handler appeared and said, "The mission is green, and we have a job to do." A small covered truck pulled up out of the night, and I knew what was in it. They carried the bomb package to a sandbagged hut next to the strip. I understood this could be serious, and I started the checklists. It was time to change into unmarked camouflaged utilities and get painted up. I was told no wetsuit would be necessary tonight. I was suiting up and checking the equipment when I noticed the air was fairly calm with that slight breeze to the north. This was again a positive sign, and I was aware of a southerly wind all day. The steam boiling from my eggs earlier in the day was blowing north, and I knew this was needed for a nuclear mission. Now mostly cloudy, it was a fairly dark night as the faint moon was waning in and out of the clouds, and the clouds were moving ever so slowly to the north. After the briefing, I was escorted to the chopper. At the time, the pilots were aboard.

With all the necessary equipment and the bomb strapped on, two Marines helped me up and into the seat on the helicopter. Time wise, it was going to be a short journey to the target site. Then a stern deep voice began shouting out, "Marine, you have a mission to do, and you will do your job. Do you understand your mission?"

"Yes, sir!"

"Do you understand thousands of Marines are depending on you?"

"Yes, sir!"

"Do you understand your job is to destroy the enemy and we're going to win this war?"

"Yes, sir!"

"Do you understand you cannot fail and you will not allow this bomb or you to be captured?"

"Yes, sir!"

"Do you understand your country is depending on you tonight?"

"Yes, sir!"

"Marine, do your job!"

"Yes, sir!"

"May God bless you, son."

The chopper started to roar and buffet. All thumbs were up! I knew the end was near.

Reality set in, and my entire life flashed in front of my eyes! I then started to fiercely concentrate; this was what all the training was about!

The refrigerated body-bag trucks were within yards of the airstrip. The blood was oozing from those trucks to the ground. The smell of death and the smell of fuel created a stench. The low-laying light fog and weather were bleak. The love for life was gone! My heart was thumping although I was trained to stay calm. With the adrenaline pounding, baseball somehow entered my mind! Playing for the New York Yankees and seeing the third brick down again in Angela's fireplace were not real anymore! Thousands of Marines' lives were all that mattered! Numb and dazed, I was relying on the repetitious and monotonous training to get me through. Suddenly, I was thankful for all I had ever experienced in life. I wrote my goodbyes and expressed my endless love to my mother and Angela. I knew death was near, and I would probably not survive! Calmness set in for the moment, and the mission was again the focus. All memories of life were a whiteout. Looking down one last time, I saw a chaplain. I wondered if he was Catholic. He was doing some hand gestures of what I thought could be last rites. At the same time, a machine gun was being locked and loaded. I was strapped into a nuclear weapon without any other ADM Marine I had ever trained with, and I was on my own. Out of nowhere, another thought appeared of being an altar boy at St. Paul's Church and School in the first grade. No God, politics, or anyone's love could stop this now. It became the sole purpose of my being. Everything was on automatic; all the ADM training made the mission as if I had done it a million times before. The training paid off; it was all so familiar. Suddenly, one last thought rushed into my head, and it seemed sort of funny. I never had a chance to experience sex in my lifetime! My thoughts then raced back to not being captured and the bomb not falling into enemy hands. Carrying a .45-caliber pistol and explosives, being captured was not an option. I was to blow the bomb up as a dirty bomb if need be and then, in the end, turn the gun on myself if there was no possible way out. On this night, I was geared up with rats, the snake, colored smoke, colored flares, a colored light gun, and a radio. I knew Morse code forward and backward. With all this equipment, I knew communications would most likely not be a concern tonight.

I fully understood, failure would result in the loss of one or more of our strategic firebases. Thousands of Marines would be slaughtered, and any public support for the war would be lost forever. LBJ would lose his presidency, and General Westmoreland would be ousted. The North Vietnamese Communist would win the war. There could be no mistakes tonight!

The chopper blades were turning faster and faster. Although the checklists were tedious, I was in lightning-fast mode when, suddenly, another order was barked out, "STAND DOWN! STAND DOWN, MARINE! EVERYONE STAND DOWN! THE MISSION IS ON A HOLD!"

The chopper started to quiet down, and I was wondering, *What the hell? Did the weather change? Did the wind change? Did the window of opportunity close for other reasons?* I yelled down to the handler, "What's happening?" He answered, "We are on hold for a minute or two." The chopper was still running, and we were told to hold our positions. I was reviewing maps and communication procedures with a penlight when I realized I was talking to myself, asking, *Why the hell are we on hold? We just can't leave our boys hanging out there!* With my adrenaline overflowing, I blurted out again, "What's going on? What's the delay?" The handler yelled back, "Settle down, Marine, and cut the crap!" I knew he was just as upset and full of angst as me, and it seemed that normal protocol was not being adhered to. Was this handler going with me, or was he staying behind? I was confused.

The front of the chopper was pointing north, and the engine was still running. From my position in the seat, I could see to the north-northwest and to the southwest looking out the door. Night illumination flares were being shot up and bursting everywhere in the distance. The backdrop of the sky to the north and west were lighting up with heavy artillery explosions from the direction of Camp Carroll and Khe Sanh from the southwest as well as Con Thien to the northwest of our position. The explosions were more than the usual artillery fire we were all accustomed to in the distance. I was thinking maybe it was our own artillery being fired to create a diversion. I also thought we could be waiting for a path to be cleared for the mission. My mouth was cotton, and it was hard to swallow. No one was talking, and we were all waiting on what was to come. The chopper had been running for over thirty minutes when the handler approached the door again. I bent over to hear him asking me if I was okay. I gave him a thumbs-up, and I yelled, "Let's turn this war around!" He backed away from the door while nodding yes.

The machine gunner turned and yelled to me, "What's in the bag?" I shook my head no. He yelled again, "What's in the sack?" This time I told him, "You'll find out in a few minutes, turn around, you're not allowed to talk to me." I then heard chatter on the radios, but I couldn't make out what was being said. The chatter continued on for several minutes, and the waiting around was hell. A few minutes later the handler approached the chopper again, looked up, and gave us both thumbs-down while yelling "It's over, it's over!" shaking his head no and now giving the sign to cut the engine. I took a deep breath and started to think this might not be my final night on earth.

There was no way to know what happened or what changed. It's just the way it was. Could it have been the Marine Corps and CIA once again making sure I was reliable, prepared, and up for the mission? With so little time left to serve in Vietnam, what would be the purpose of all this now? Every drill had a different place and twist to it, each designed to make me believe it was real, but why now? If this was a drill, why would it include a meaningless delay and holding period? The timing and nature of a drill now made no sense at all. I thought then it was real, and there was nothing to make me believe otherwise today. The bomb package was strapped on, and once again it was taken off and away.

Nov. 1967

Dear Mother

If you recieve this letter it means I did not suffer and I have vanished from earth not to be found. I'd like for you to believe I'm in heaven.

Please know it was for a cause way bigger than me. Please pray for me and please be patient. In time you will surely know what happened.

Your Loving Son
Michael

Transcript of letter and picture of Michael falling asleep with his boots on after writing letters.

(Picture courtesy of Michael Chapanar.)

Dear Mother,

If you receive this letter, it means I did not suffer and I have vanished from earth not to be found. I'd like for you to believe I'm in heaven. Please know it was for a cause way bigger than me. Please pray for me and please be patient. In time you will surely know what happened. Your loving son, Michael

Nov. 1967

Angela my Love

I know you pray for me everyday, Angela my Love please say an extra Prayer for me. If you are reading this letter it means I'm no longer in this world. You may be comforted to know I had one last job to do that was allot more important than one person. You may also be Comforted knowing I did not suffer.

Angela, while on this earth you were my destiny. It seems now I was destined to help my brother Marines and pherhaps help save our Country from prolonging this terrible War. I will always Love You.

Michael

Transcript of letter written to Angela

Angela my Love,

I know you pray for me every day. Angela my love please say an extra prayer for me. If you are reading this letter it means I'm no longer in this world. You may be comforted to know I had one last job to do that was a lot more important than one person. You may also be comforted knowing I did not suffer. Angela, while on this earth you were my destiny. It seems now, I was destined to help my brother Marines and perhaps help save our country from prolonging this terrible war. I will always love you. Michael

CHAPTER 30

The Debriefing

It seemed now combat was over for me. I was set to wait out the remaining days in Dong Ha. My tour in Nam was coming to an end. The transfer orders to go home were in. It was about going home now. My dreams were starting up again. Life was once again in front of me. Each minute left in Nam was like an hour. Anxiety was overwhelming, and it was hard to believe I was going to make it out alive—actually going home to be a free man in America, see the third brick down, and marry Angela.

I was tired. Everything in my head was a blur. I needed a rest, a good sleep, and everything would be okay, just fine. I kept asking myself if the past twelve months were real or just a nightmare and wondering how all this would go on without me. I found myself focusing on the young Marine boys just arriving to Vietnam and the young men who still had a few months left before going home. Knowing many of these young men would never return home was very claustrophobic. There was not much more I could do. I wanted to hug each one of them and wish Godspeed.

That night I tried to get some sleep, but caught only a few winks at a time. Too many thoughts were flowing through my head— thoughts of not being home for a year and a half and exactly what I was going to talk about when I got there. *What am I going to do first? How am I going to act when I first see Angela, and will she still love me? Will my mom and dad be proud? What will my two younger brothers be thinking? Will I ever be a normal person again, and what will the country think of me?*

A few days later I was cutting hair although very few Marines were coming in the shop, and it was a long day. Several artillery rounds landed inside our perimeter that morning—nothing too close, and I received word no one was hurt. That night the sounds of war were rumbling on, but I managed to get some sleep. I was actually getting accustomed to the idea of going home. I woke up wondering what it was going to feel like leaving Dong Ha for the last time, then Da Nang Air Base, and finally, Vietnam. Was it really going to happen?

I was packing up a few things between haircuts and wanted to sneak a couple of items home, maybe an empty cartridge belt or my cloth helmet liner with the word *Angela* written on it.

Around 3:00 p.m. a jeep pulled up, and the driver said he was here to take me to the airstrip. I was excited; maybe I was going home earlier than expected. When we arrived at the airstrip, I saw a different handler standing there, waiting for me. Seeing him there jolted me. I couldn't imagine why this guy would be here now.

I walked up to him, and he had a different look on his face—a look I had never seen before, and he said those words, "Michael, we have a job to do." There was a sandbagged tent a few yards away. He said, "Come with me." We entered the tent, and he told me we needed to talk. "I must debrief you." I started to gather my composure as the conversation began. "First, I want to say, you did a hell of a job. I also want to inform you that two replacements have now arrived here in Dong Ha. I don't believe you ever wavered, and you kept your mouth shut. Going forward must be just as airtight. No leaking! A leak could jeopardize a future mission and our effort in the war. We know you have a woman waiting. She must never know even if you marry her. I understand, your parents served in the United States Navy, they must never know, and you can't tell your two younger brothers either. There can be absolutely no discussion of nuclear war or any of your highly classified activities. I don't want to make unwarranted threats although any leak will absolutely not be tolerated. Do you understand, we (the CIA) have eyes and ears everywhere?" I said, "Yes, I understand." We stood up, shook hands, and said, "So long." I left the tent relieved.

The jeep was waiting to take me back when I noticed a chaplain/priest bending over a body bag near the refrigerated body-bag trucks. I walked over to him; he didn't recognize me. I introduced myself and asked if he was, by chance, here at about two in the morning several nights ago. He said yes and asked how I knew. I explained to him that I was aboard the helicopter that night with a package strapped on. He looked grim and said, "You may thank the Lord it never took off." He performed the sign of the cross, and I said, "Thank you, Father." We shook hands, and I left him attending to our dead.

Upon returning to the barbershop, there was a Marine waiting for a haircut. It was the Marine I told to mail the letters addressed to my mother and Angela if I did not return or was killed a couple of nights earlier. He sat in the barber chair, pulled out the two letters, and said, "I don't think I will need to mail these" and handed them back to me. Both letters were still sealed shut.

CHAPTER 31

My Last Convoy

A few days later I found it difficult to wrap my head around the fact I was being called away from the barbershop area and being sent out on the front lines once again. It was not going to be another day in the barbershop, cutting hair and dreaming of going home. Marines not presently out in the field were being summoned to report to the motor pool. There was an urgent need for a supply convoy to Con Thien. A newly appointed sergeant entered the barbershop, and I was thinking he came in for a haircut, but I was mistaken and surprised by his demand. The sergeant knew I would be an asset doing minesweeping and clearing the way if there were problems, so I was ordered to go on the convoy.

After being removed from minesweeping duties for only a few months, I found it hard to focus on the task assigned. I had not worked with mines, trip wires, or booby traps for what seemed like an eternity and had no premonition of ever doing so again. The ADM replacements were now in Dong Ha, and I had finally been relieved of nuclear weapon responsibilities, blissfully thinking I did all that was asked. With only days and hours left, I awoke each remaining morning, touching my face and legs, wondering how I was still in one piece. I promised myself I would never go home disfigured. I knew I didn't have the guts to make it through life that way yet, I also felt Angela would accept me as long as I made it home to her. The nightmare of witnessing others going home with missing limbs was etched in my mind. Up to that morning it looked like I might make it home intact. How could I go out one more time and get away with it? A cruel answer kept entering my mind. I didn't understand, it was just another flip of the coin and no different than any other time that came before. The promises I made to Jesus were so many that no human being could fulfill them all. I was now thinking this last trip outside the gates of Dong Ha was going to be the convoy that would get me wounded. Would I lose my legs, arms, or life itself?

Before leaving I strolled out to the barbershop and sat in the barber chair that had served so well. I was wondering if the skid of unused body bags that just arrived contained the one bag that would hold my remains. Even a cat had only nine lives.

Once again I tried concentrating on the third brick down in Angela's fireplace to stay calm, but this time the fireplace had a fire in it, and I saw the brick burning in hell. The most pleasant thought I conjured up that morning was a bullet piercing the center of my skull and not feeling what hit me. Knowing I was unexpectantly being called out one last time, I was no longer capable of thinking pleasant thoughts.

Two Ontos track vehicles with their six recoilless rifles and two tanks with 90-mm howitzers on them were our chaperones for the day. I was not about to let anything bad happen to our escorts. I knew we were going to have air support on what looked to be a fairly sunny day. The gung ho Marines who just recently entered on the Vietnam scene were anxious to jump in their trucks and head out. I had to remain unshaken and confident in front of them. How could I let these baby-faced, innocent kids down? Feeling like an older brother, knowing some of them outranked me, I barked out, "Okay, devil dogs, let's roll on." I was now the veteran Marine who knew all the tricks of the trade and had sensed their respect. I was fortunate to receive some special on-the-job training from other veteran combat Marines when I first arrived in Nam. They cared and gave their precious time and knowledge. I soaked it up like a sponge and always made an effort to pass on my experiences whenever possible.

In a mysterious way situational awareness is a sixth sense. You either have it, or you don't although with years of experience it can be acquired. Most catchers in baseball know what I'm referring too. It's a unique ability to size up ten things at one time while not getting fixated on any one thing. Catchers do this when behind the plate in baseball games. It's the reason they make good managers. The catcher must feel, hear, and analyze what is taking place in many different situations. He knows what's happening at every position with each player. Yet his primary focus is on his pitcher, the batter, the bullpen, and the next batter up. Somehow it all becomes second nature, and while baseball is just a game, war is not. This inherent ability of situational awareness is essential in war, or you're dead.

With just a few days left in that hellhole, the convoy started out slowly and advanced about four miles when we were suddenly called into action. The wet and treacherous road ahead, with all its twists and turns, did not look passable. The rubble of bricks and concrete from a church lay along the deteriorated path. As I jumped off the truck to observe the debris, I spotted a thin wire reflecting in the sunlight across our path, attached to the concrete. With scrutiny we began determining what lay ahead. Equipped with a mine detector in one hand and a trip-wire feeler and probing rod in the other, I was moving slowly and carefully trying to determine what needed to be done when I spotted multiple trip wires in several areas. I also noticed the path ahead was recently disturbed. The hamlet we passed less than seventy-five yards back was too quiet and didn't look normal. The birds were avoiding the area, and there were no dogs barking or animals moving around. There were no children to be found anywhere, and it was as if the entire area was hunkered down, waiting. I then spotted enemy markers pointing to some suspicious-looking areas. It was looking too dangerous as the captain started to slowly move the convoy in reverse. We were all using hand signals to communicate and sensed the enemy was listening and watching. The commander quietly approached and asked what I thought. I gave him my assessment of our predicament and said even if we cleared this section of the road, it was not looking much better ahead. It's going to take time to clear, and we would be in the dark before we got to our destination. There were too many negative signs everywhere. I motioned to our lead vehicle to bring up a Polaroid camera, and I snapped a few close-up pictures to analyze with the captain. It looked as if the trip wires were not the only problem. There was a thin electrical wire showing up on one of the Polaroid pictures. This indicated we were looking at an electronic command device with possibly someone lying in wait to detonate it precisely at the right moment. Suddenly, we both spotted a black cobra snake darting out of the cement rubble, crossing the path ahead of us. We looked at each other, and I asked the commander just how vital was this cargo we were transporting up to Con Thien. He said, "Not that vital, let's get the hell out of here!" It was settled—the convoy had gone as far as possible and needed to turn around and get back to base before dark. As the convoy went backward toward Dong Ha, one Ontos briefly held its position until the rest of us were cleared of its backblast area. The Ontos then fired two of its six recoilless rifles into the cement rubble debris. The explosions were enormous and much greater than two rounds from the Ontos would have produced. Everyone instantly knew the Ontos rounds hit something much larger than a booby-trapped mine, avoiding a major disaster. Our attention turned to the trip back, and we realized it would be just as daunting as it was going up. Approximately two hours later we were approaching the Dong Ha base. We heard the sound of artillery rounds roaring high overhead, hoping our convoy would not be their next target. Finally, with the base in sight, the artillery sounds quieted down, and my heart stopped pounding. I couldn't express emotion to other Marines although I was a wreck inside, visualizing all that took place that day. My confidence level and mental capacity were both completely drained from my system, and even my knees were knocking. I was empty inside, and my boots were shaking as well. My mind was shattered even more when I spoke to the few Marines that night who were ordered to go on this mission. I found these Marines had very little demolition training. Most had little sense of situational awareness with no combat experience.

Later that night after settling down, I acted like a college professor. I spent the next several hours illustrating to our rookie Marines what we all needed to watch out for that day. Everyone was listening intently and had many questions. Months earlier I put up about a dozen Polaroid pictures on the shrapnel-ridden tin wall in the barbershop. I had taken the pictures to further analyze the various types of booby traps, mines, and wires we had crossed paths with on previous assignments. I let each Marine pick the one they wanted to keep.

There was quite a change in attitude from that morning to that night. As it turned out, it was one of a few rewarding nights I spent in Nam. The comradery of all the guys made it so good. We were safe and sound, and no one was hurt that day. If I could have only shared some nuclear weapon training stories with them. Maybe these guys were developing their own sixth sense. I was certainly hoping so as I crossed off another day on my calendar.

CHAPTER 32

Bizarre Happenings

On December 5, 1965, less than one year prior to my arrival in Vietnam, an incident at sea took place near Okinawa. An A-4 Skyhawk attack jet rolled off the aircraft carrier *USS Ticonderoga* into sixteen thousand feet of water, resulting in the loss of the pilot, the aircraft, and believe it or not, the B43 nuclear bomb it was carrying, all of which were too deep for recovery. Since the ship was traveling to Japan from duty in the Vietnam war zone, no public mention was made of the incident, and it would not come to light until 1981 when a Pentagon report revealed that a one-megaton bomb had been lost. It has me guessing how much official protocol was or was not strictly adhered to per the manual during this extreme operation aboard the *Ticonderoga* ship.

* * *

In December 2015, the United States government acknowledged officially for the first time that it had stored nuclear weapons in Okinawa prior to 1972. This fact had been widely speculated since the '60s. It could never be said that Daniel Ellsberg and Robert McNamara were not aware of these types of highly classified secrets.

* * *

Major General Bruno A. Hochmuth, commanding general, Third Marine Division, personally signed the Division Special Order #441-67. The order was a permanent change of station, sending me home from Vietnam and back to the United States of America. I left Vietnam for the last time on November 22, 1967. One week before I left for home, our leader and the man who signed my order, Major General Bruno A. Hochmuth, was killed on November 14, 1967.

The general was in a helicopter on his way to Dong Ha at approximately one thousand five hundred feet high, doing about ninety knots airspeed, some thirty miles below the DMZ, when his helicopter mysteriously exploded in midair. The chopper erupted into a ball of fire spewing dense, black smoke while falling to the earth in a near-vertical descent. All five Marines on board were killed. How did this happen when it was said no shot had been fired? Lieutenant General R. E. Cushman Jr. and Major General Hochmuth were close personal friends. General Cushman went to the scene of the crash to see where his friend had perished. In the eight months of his command, Hochmuth directed his leath-ernecks in dozens of major operations includ-ing some of the roughest of the war along the DMZ. It was a bad day for Marines on the DMZ and the Marine Corps. Our leader had been killed.

Major General Bruno A. Hochmuth
(official USMC photo).

Looking back, was it possible General Hochmuth had something to do with not carrying out my mission to its conclusion? Although it didn't seem so, I believed his untimely death took place at a time when a lot of senseless things were going on. How was it that a general in charge of the Third

Marine Division in Vietnam, along with five other Marines, mysteriously blew up in a helicopter? Pretty bizarre!

* * *

How would I ever know if what I had strapped on was a real nuclear weapon? I would never know unless I'd seen the flash, and then I wouldn't have known for long! My job was to stay mentally and physically ready to deploy the weapon in any conceivable condition.

The mission was far beyond the call, and we were totally prepared to carry it out. Marines fought for our flag since well before my time. How could any combat Marine turn down the duty to save other Marines?

After twelve months of combat, it was hard to comprehend how I was so blessed to make it when so many others were either killed or maimed terribly. Those people were real heroes.

From the onset, October 1966, of ADM training in San Diego, I was not exempt from occasional gruesome thoughts and nightmares of the bomb actually going off. Encountering these nightmares while serving in Vietnam was more disconcerting. There was no way to confide in anyone regarding the nightmarish and claustrophobic events. I was very concerned I could unknowingly talk in my sleep, but to the best of my knowledge no talking ever occurred. Another ghastly image I visualized was being captured by enemy forces while in possession of the nuclear weapon. If the horrific dream woke me up, I'd quickly turn my attention to the third brick down. Thank God, the third brick down took me home to America and put me back to sleep most of the time. Any thoughts of other normal things going on in the rest of the world were clouded.

In the fall of 1967 in Dong Ha, I was listening to a baseball game on a transoceanic radio in the barbershop. The Boston Red Sox were playing for a world championship, and at the time five hundred thousand kids were fighting for their existence in Vietnam.

We heard racial tensions were heating up in America, but never did I see a situation where the skin color of a Marine—whether white, black, Asian, or Hispanic—was a consideration, certainly not on the DMZ in 1967. We were all American Marines watching out for one another. Each had moms, dads, brothers, sisters, and girlfriends or wives waiting for us. We loved life, and we all had people who loved us. The most important endeavor in my life was fighting for the greatest nation on the planet; after all, our country is and always will be God's greatest gift to humanity.

CHAPTER 33

Absent without Leave—AWOL

Although brokenhearted and feeling down, I went on to leave Vietnam on November 22. It was a twenty-three-hour trip to the Marine Corps Air Station El Toro in California. This was supposed to be a happy flight, but because of General Hochmuth's death, it was a somber one and took a lot of enthusiasm out of going home.

A rumor had it that if you got back to the United States with fifty-nine days or less to serve on active duty, you would be granted an early-out discharge. With sixty days or more left to serve on active duty, you would have to serve out your remaining sixty days.

My first day of active duty was January 25, 1966. The last day of my two-year active duty obligation was to be on January 24, 1968. By all calculations I would land in the United States with possibly sixty-one days left and would have to serve out my two-year obligation.

So I developed plan B. My uncle John lived in Vista, California. I thought if I could go over the hill and get lost for a couple of days and return with fifty-nine days or less to serve, I would get the early out.

When we landed at El Toro, I was told to get in the line with sixty days or more left to serve. The gunnery sergeant looked at my orders and papers and said, "Marine, you must serve out your two-year obligation." I was sent to the unhappy line!

I was forced to implement plan B. I inched my seabag toward an exit door of the giant building and rolled a full, shook-up, unopened can of Coke across the floor of the processing center. It hit the wall and created a diversion! The can exploded. It sent soda all over the place, and out the exit on the other side of the building I went, seabag and all. It was the last thing I ever blew up in the Marine Corps.

Very calmly, I found a phone booth and called Uncle John. I asked him to come pick me up. He was an hour from El Toro. When he showed up, I said I needed to put my sea-bag in his trunk. I hopped into his trunk along with the seabag, yelling out my plan to get lost for two days. It was perfect. He started the car, and we left the base. Uncle John was also a little ornery, and he was laughing.

Two days later we returned to the exact same spot; I grabbed the seabag and said, "I love you" and goodbye.

When the next plane from Vietnam landed, I blended in with one hundred fifty

Marines getting off the plane, celebrating, yelling, and kissing the ground. I ended up being the last person sitting in the processing center that day. I was sitting there, pretending to be waiting for my name to be called. But I was obviously not on the manifest list. Being the only one left, the gunny said, "Who the hell are you? You are not on my list. When did you get here?" I said, "I got in on the last plane with everyone else." The gunny reviewed my papers and took his time about it; he looked puzzled! Finally, he said, "You have fifty-nine days left. Go over to the 'fifty-nine days and less' table, you're going to be discharged." As I started walking away from him, he said, "Marine, I should send your ass to the brig." I gave him a befuddled look and kept walking!

Finally, he yelled, "Marine!" I abruptly stopped, and he said, "Thank you for your service in Vietnam." I started to breathe again and gave him a thumbs-up!

And that's how I served only twenty-two months on active duty in the USMC. It took a little more than ten days to process out.

December 7 is the anniversary of the Japanese attack on Pearl Harbor in 1941. Ironically, twenty-six years later, on December 7 I was discharged. It was another coincidental and significant date in my life. When I hopped on the plane to come home, I was required to wear my uniform in order to fly for free. I wore the dress-green uniform for the last time, boarding the plane. Thirty minutes into the flight, I changed into the pinstriped suit and tie I had purchased while on the last ADM training trip to Okinawa in July. It was perfect! I was the last one to get off the plane in Canton. Angela and her future two bridesmaids were waiting at the bottom of the steps. I strutted down the steps of the plane like a well-groomed business-man. Of course, I knew absolutely nothing about business and had very little money. Yet it all added up to the best kiss in my life at the bottom of the steps. I made it home, and she was waiting. Another significant date in my life is November 10, the Marine Corps birthday; November 10 is also Angela's birthday.

CHAPTER 34

Westmoreland's BS

A few days after returning to the United States on November 23, I caught wind of a speech General Westmoreland concocted several days earlier. The general put forth an important address to the National Press Club on November 21. He explained how his war of attrition was working. He said the end was in view, and the war was now entering into its final phase. Why would Westmoreland say such gibberish in his analysis when just weeks earlier my mission was more eminent than ever? Because of inclement weather and a massive buildup of enemy strength in and around the DMZ area, I was ordered to be ready for deployment with the bomb. The scenario being painted at the press club and the current situation in Vietnam did not match up. Other than misleading the American people for political purposes, it made no sense at all. If General Westmoreland's war plans were looking successful and we were making great progress as he stated, why would he have the idea of using a nuclear weapon to send Hanoi a message, killing thousands of people in the process? Westmoreland was aware President Johnson and Secretary of Defense McNamara realized his war of attrition was not working. Johnson and McNamara also knew the speech was only given to serve their political objectives. All three of them were purposely misleading the American public. Less than ten weeks later their hogwash of winning anything was proven just that, *hogwash*. It goes to show, the platform of false prophets is a crowded one.

* * *

Just prior to leaving Vietnam for home, the intel from reliable sources said something entirely different. During my last trip to Okinawa in July, I was informed the enemy strength was increasing throughout all of South Vietnam.

My mother, who was in constant contact with Mary Jane Vann, kept me updated on any news regarding John Vann. In a concerted letter written in the fall of '67, Mother wrote and said John was pissed off and did not believe we were winning. Mary Jane said John was not thrilled with where the war was headed. Obviously, the CIA handler in Vietnam knew my mission was only going to happen if we were being overwhelmed by enemy strength. Throughout the fall months, the handler was becoming more adamant each day that our mission was going to be carried out. The sources I had available to me were all on the same page. We were getting our ass kicked in Vietnam, and something needed to change. Did we need more men and more bombs, or were we going to use a nuclear weapon? These were questions the United States needed to answer quickly.

I figured my outgoing letters were always being censored. Angela would let me know when part of a letter I sent to her or Mother was cut out and monitored. Apparently and unknowingly, I mentioned a few things the USMC or CIA did not want sent home. Therefore, I could not express my opinion on how the war was going and what I was privy too. Incoming mail sent to me was never tampered with as far as I knew.

CHAPTER 35

Out and About

On January 30, 1968, I was, of course, out of the Marine Corps and was sitting in a local restaurant, Kimm Inn, with a couple of buddies after work. I had the owner, Zack, convinced I was twenty-one years old and could have a beer. I would not be twenty-one until April 26. On each side of the restaurant/bar were TVs. I was looking up at the breaking news when the restaurant was overcome with silence as patrons were stunned. The North Vietnamese Army and the Viet Cong were attempting to overrun the entire country of South Vietnam. I was not as startled as other patrons to see what was happening. Rather than startled, I was angered, feeling guilty and partially responsible. The televised report was proof we were not winning the war of attrition, and I felt the American people were being deceived and misled. It seemed we gave North Vietnam the opportunity to launch the Tet Offensive attacks, and all our wounded, maimed, and killed in 1967 might have been in vain.

I couldn't explain to anyone what we accomplished in '67, and I knew we were not winning the war by any means. We didn't do what was necessary to prevent the Tet Offensive, and it put me in a state of depression. Meanwhile, my fiancée, Angela, had no idea how I was feeling. She was busy working and planning our upcoming wedding on May 4. The entire war was now behind her, but not yet for me. Angela had no idea what I did in Vietnam and what I was trained to do. I was concerned, if she somehow found out, she would think I was a cruel, inhumane person and would not want to marry me. She didn't understand why I was so down and depressed when in her mind I should have been happy to be home and alive.

I was now living with a nuclear-weapon secret, knowing we could have stopped the Tet Offensive and maybe even ended the war. We didn't get it right, and we were now going to lose the remaining support from the American people.

I actually had thoughts of going back to Vietnam, but I was too discouraged trying to make sense of it all. I couldn't even bring myself to accept how I made it out alive the first time. It was hard to understand how I was ever going to be happy in life again. Being around Angela a few hours a day was what I needed to feel human again with hope for the future.

I couldn't have a conversation about the war in general because people didn't want to hear about it. Those who did talk politics ended up fighting and hating one another. The race riots, drug problems, and the Vietnam War had everyone at one another's throat. Three assassinations in a span of five years (President John F. Kennedy, Martin Luther King, and Robert F. Kennedy), 1963–1968, put America on the brink. When people found out I was a combat Marine who served in Vietnam, I was branded an outcast.

Turning all my attention to Angela was my only salvation. I knew I needed to keep Angela and her mother from somehow finding out about my training to annihilate masses of Asian people. If I lost Angela, my life was over.

I cried myself to sleep countless nights, thinking about how to go on, but in the end my prayers were miraculously answered.

Angela, pictured below, was exactly where I dreamed she would be—in her living room, standing next to the third brick down, anxiously waiting. Angela and I were married on May 4, 1968. The wedding was marvelous, and the honeymoon, even better. We've been together since that glorious day, helping each other live life happily ever after.

May 4, 1968, our wedding day.

(Pictures courtesy of Michael Chapanar.)

CHAPTER 36

The MOS 1372 Replacements Were Killed

On October 5, 1966, Robert E. Cushman Jr., the commanding general of Camp Pendleton, personally signed the orders that sent me to North Island San Diego Nuclear Weapons Training Center on October 9, 1966. It was the start of an ongoing process of elimination of the few Marines who were chosen to train with and deploy a tactical nuclear weapon. Surviving that process was a mental and physical challenge in itself. I still have the orders in my possession today.

In June of 1967 General Cushman became commanding general of the Third Marine Amphibious Force in Vietnam and was awarded the largest combined combat unit ever led by a U.S. Marine. I also have the secret microfiche orders sending me from Vietnam to Okinawa three times for ADM training and intelligence briefings.

Then in 1969 Cushman was named deputy director of the CIA, serving in that position until 1972. Robert E. Cushman Jr. was eventually promoted again on January 1, 1972, to commandant of the Marine Corps.

(Picture courtesy of USMC History Division.)

Several months after his appearance in the October '67 CBS special news report, *General Cushman* played a significant role in implementing the abandonment of the most important base on the DMZ. The *forces* he referred to in the CBS report that could be brought to bear in defense of the area were obviously never totally brought to bear, the *forces* being a tactical nuclear weapon.

Consequently, the dismantling of Khe Sanh began on June 19, 1968; on July 5 it was complete. Nothing visual was left to indicate that the Americans had been forced to withdraw. Eight hundred bunkers, miles of barbed wire, and acres of metal runway materials were buried, destroyed, or physically removed. For the Marines who fought at Khe Sanh, I was left wondering why I was not given the final order to carry out the mission. While it might have ultimately cost me my life, we desperately needed to save the base and, for that matter, the war. Perhaps, the thirty-minute turning point and the eventual outcome of the war was the night we had the chopper running and ready to fly. I was aboard, strapped to a nuclear bomb, waiting for the final signal to take off. It would have certainly changed the war as we knew it. A timely opportunity to send the message to Hanoi and, perhaps, end the war had passed.

* * *

The ADM Marines were killed

The two ADM replacements my CIA handler referred to in my debriefing were now in Dong Ha, Vietnam. I was relieved of all nuclear weapon responsibilities. As per Form NAVMC 118 (11), my security clearance and reliability billet, as defined in MCO 5510.7, were terminated because of my transfer home. Unfortunately, the two ADM replacements were killed. Tribute pages and their pictures can be found online by simply entering their ranks and names. A tribute to Sergeant Irwin Lee Knickerbocker, MOS 1372 ADM, was created by Dr. J and maintained by Tony. Sgt. Knickerbocker arrived in Vietnam on November 14, 1967. He was tragically killed when a 130-mm enemy artillery round hit the Dong Ha mess hall.

A tribute to Corporal Michael Lawrence Succi, MOS 1372 ADM, was created and is owned by Staff Sergeant Michael Yager. Corporal Michael Succi arrived in Vietnam on November 12, 1967. He was sadly killed a few miles outside of Dong Ha, clearing mines in the Cam Lo area (refer to map B, p. 24). I never had the honor of meeting Michael or Irwin. Both Marines were brave young men who were given opportunities to fight for the freedom of others. They are two American heroes; may their souls rest in peace.

* * *

General Westmoreland, in 1984, brought a $120-million libel suit against CBS in connection with a 1982 documentary, "The Uncounted Enemy: A Vietnam Deception." The documentary said that General Westmoreland's command had blocked reports from officers in its combined intelligence center, regarding approximately twenty-five thousand North Vietnamese troops who were infiltrating into South Vietnam each month in the fall of 1967. Lieutenant General Phillip B. Davidson Jr. was head of military intelligence in South Vietnam in 1967. General Davidson testified in 1984 that there was usually a six-month time lag before most intelligence officers would know the magnitude of infiltration for a particular month. Davidson further said he and other ranking officers learned as early as November 1967 that a total of twenty-five thousand North Vietnamese were moving southward toward Khe Sanh, but the source of the information was highly secret communications intelligence from the National Security Agency (NSA.) General Davidson went on to say this information was not normally shared with officers in the combined intelligence center because Vietnamese worked there.

It was well-known that a debate was raging at the time over the subject of enemy strength with General Westmoreland's command and the Central Intelligence Agency. The CIA, like some military intelligence analysts in Saigon, wanted to increase the estimate of enemy strength to as much as five hundred thousand. It was pointed out that General Davidson had given instructions to a subordinate in August 1967 that read, "This headquarters will not accept a figure in excess of the current strength figure carried by the press," which was set at about three hundred thousand.

Secretary of Defense Robert McNamara stressed his growing disenchantment with the military reporting from Vietnam. McNamara said, "You could not reconcile the number of the enemy, the level of infiltration, the body count, and the resultant figures. It just didn't add up. I never did get a good answer because there weren't any answers."

McNamara was said to have believed infiltration by the North Vietnamese troops into the south was much larger than reports indicated. In a deposition, he stated, "It could have been substantially higher by a factor of two or three or ten."

On February 18, 1985, Westmoreland dropped his $120-million libel suit against CBS. Mr. Westmoreland ended his lawsuit, and it was dismissed without any award, retraction, or apology from CBS. He also agreed to pay his own legal fees.

As author of this book, I must say there was an abundance of deception going on in the fall of 1967. It is my opinion that ego and politics were now the driving forces of the war from that time period forward. No one wanted to be the first person in United States history to lose a foreign war. I believe the question I posed on page 22 of this book is a worthy one: When ego and deceit replace logic and truth in war, who on earth is *beyond the call* of destruction?

CHAPTER 37

Hello World

On our second wedding anniversary, May 4, 1970, the Ohio National Guard shot and killed four Kent State University students and wounded nine others. Once again, I watched the horror unfold on TV just forty-five minutes north of our hometown in Canton, Ohio. It was heartbreaking to watch college kids dying at the hands of our own military. The country was being torn apart again. It was the most terrible of times for the United States. I thought our nation would never heal.

The war blazed on for several more years with little hope of winning. Angela kept telling me we must put the war behind us. We must live our own lives. We were somehow managing to do that although I was constantly taking a verbal pasting from the flower children, peaceniks, and their peace chiefs. Kent State University was thirty-five miles from our hometown with an off-campus branch of the university less than three miles from our home in Canton. I was the store manager with the Zales Jewelry Diamond Company for their store in Kent, Ohio, which was located two miles from the Kent State Main Campus. It was, by far, the best job I ever had, and the store was doing large amounts of business with the college kids. When getting engaged or married, it was the store for their diamond ring. Zales thought they hired the right manager for the job—a former Marine with no criminal record. My personality was outgoing and friendly, and selling diamonds was clean and fun.

I loved the job, and we were selling a lot of diamonds. For some reason, in the months to follow, there was an unusual amount of returns compared to other Zales stores. When the college kids in Kent found out they purchased a diamond ring for life from a Vietnam combat veteran who was currently in the Marine Corps Reserve, serving out his six-year obligation, it was too much, and back came the diamond. The situation was inexplicable to Zales regional management, and I knew my job was in jeopardy. All other manager positions with Zales in Ohio were filled with career managers, and there were no other stores in Ohio I could transfer to as manager. I was hoping Zales would not put two and two together and find out the returns were because of my military background. Most of the college kids financed the purchase of their diamond ring, and upon return, the transaction had to be completely reversed. A few of my employees were catching on, and the word was filtering back to regional management. Zales gave me the option to quit. In the end I had no choice, but to quit. It was hard to explain to my beautiful wife, and I started some hard drinking. At the time she was a secretary with Ohio Power Company and still working at her first job in life. We just couldn't cut it on her salary alone, and unemployment benefits were not available because I quit the job. The Vietnam War was still haunting us, and I was totally unaware, by quitting the job, I would become ineligible for unemployment benefits. Zales neglected to tell me I would be ineligible for unemployment benefits, and I was unemployed with no income. That's when my friend Roger entered my life once again. He heard I was unemployed and called to see how I was doing. He mentioned his boss was looking for a recruit in the investment and insurance business.

I was hired, and for the next thirty years I was busy helping families invest and plan for their children's college education as well as preparing for their own retirement, at the same time making sure they had a life insurance policy that would handle their family's needs in case of premature death. Angela went on to work for the local school districts as an administrative secretary until retirement. She also helped with unseen war injuries my entire life. We have one daughter, Yvette, and two grandchildren, Mia and Max.

Although life and war injuries tripped me up on the path to a possible professional baseball career, at age forty-nine I found myself once again behind home plate. In 1997 our team won the National Amateur Baseball Championship at Lee County Minnesota Twins Spring Training Stadium in

Fort Myers, Florida. Our Canton, Ohio team named "Grand Slam" won the Roy Hobbs AA Baseball World Series title. The following year our team made it back to the World Series and it was an honor to be selected Most Valuable Player (MVP). With Angela and daughter, Yvette, in the stands both years, my dreams were fulfilled.

CHAPTER 38

The Soldier of the Vietnam War Is Dead

In the spring of 1972 Mother and Uncle George were preparing to fly to Washington; Mother knew it was going to be a tear-jerking, somber trip. A family member died in Vietnam. John Paul Vann was killed when his helicopter crashed and burned on a rainy and foggy night just outside of Kon Tum in the Central Highlands of South Vietnam (refer to map C, p. 25). John was being laid to rest at Arlington National Cemetery on June 16, 1972.

Upon arrival in Washington, Mother and George were met by family, friends, and other high-ranking dignitaries including Edward Kennedy.

Mother looked on as John Vann's flag-draped coffin was being rolled down the center aisle in the chapel on a wheeled frame. Eight pallbearers in double file were following. Mother and George were in tears; it was chilling and beyond emotional.

Daniel Ellsberg was also emotionally observing the funeral procession unfold when he recognized five of the pallbearers. The first prominent person he recognized was General Westmoreland, who walked at the front of the line. He then recognized General Bruce Palmer, vice chief of staff, who walked alongside Westmoreland. General Palmer and Westmoreland were followed by Lieutenant General Richard Stilwell and William Colby of the CIA. Stilwell was deputy commanding general of the Third Marine Amphibious Force in Vietnam in 1968. Ellsberg also recognized a fifth pallbearer, Robert Komer, who was a former CIA officer and general of the pacification campaign—a campaign the newspapers called the other war in Vietnam. Komer delivered the eulogy. It was a funeral, and they all came to pay their respects.

At the funeral reception that night Uncle George was explaining to several generals that his nephew was unable to fly and, therefore, unable to attend. At the time, I was suffering from an acute flare-up of hyperacusis (sensitive hearing), and it was not possible to get on a jet. The condition was brought on because of all the terrible sounds of war in Vietnam. Marines were not aware or told how a concussion blast and the deafening sound of an explosion could do so much future damage. Today I believe the military uses muchneeded ear protection when possible. After the funeral, just prior to the reception, the immediate family proceeded to the White House and into the Oval Office, where the president read the following citation, praising Vann:

> Soldier of peace and patriot of two nations, the name of John Paul Vann will be honored as long as free men remember the struggle to preserve the independence of South Vietnam. His military and civilian service in Vietnam spanned a decade, marked throughout by resourcefulness, professional excellence, and unsurpassed courage, by supreme dedication and personal sacrifice. A truly noble American, a superb leader, he stands with

Lafayette in that gallery of heroes who have made other brave peoples' cause their own.

President Nixon then presented to John Paul Vann's firstborn son, John Allen Vann, the Presidential Medal of Freedom. Technically, John Paul Vann was a civilian at the time of his death. This medal was the highest honor by law that could be bestowed upon a civilian.

Official White House Photo

The official White House photo was taken on June 16, 1972, in the Oval Office after the funeral. From left to right are Aaron Frank Vann Jr., Eugene Wallace Vann, Dorothy Lee Vann Cadorette, Jesse Vann, Thomas Vann, Peter Vann, Mary Jane Vann, President Richard Nixon, John Allen Vann, Secretary of Defense Melvin Laird, and to the far right, Secretary of State William Rogers.[17]

After the funeral, at the reception that evening, Uncle George was telling World War I stories to anyone who would listen, including Edward Kennedy. Then George spotted General Westmoreland talking to several other generals in attendance. Somehow George jumped in the conversation and was telling his World War I stories. At five-foot, four-inches tall, George was not easily seen in the crowd by my mother. Finally, Mother

---

[17] Neil Sheehan, *A Bright Shining Lie* (USA: Random House Inc., 1988).

located him now talking to Westmoreland regarding his nephew who served in Vietnam.

He was bragging about how his U.S. Marine Corps nephew had seen action on the DMZ and had something to do with a nuclear weapon. Uncle George probably knew more than he should have. After all, I had to tell somebody. I wonder if he ever secretly told my mother. If he did, Mother never spoke to me about it. I also always wondered if John Paul Vann had something to do with me being chosen for the secret assignments.

When Mother found him talking to Westmoreland, she proceeded to put him on a leash, leading him back to the table with Mary Jane Vann and her children. Daniel Ellsberg was also sitting at the same table next to my mother.

Before being dragged off, Westmoreland asked George, "What was your nephew's name?" George replied, "Michael Chapanar."

According to George, the general nodded his head, winked, and stated, "I know the name."

(Top picture) John Paul's son, John Allen Vann; Michael's mother, Jeanne; Daniel Ellsberg; and George, taken at the reception. (Bottom picture) Michael's mother, Jeanne; Michael and Uncle George.

(Picture Courtesy of Michael Chapanar.)

CHAPTER 39

A Nuclear War Planner

In Westmoreland's mind Khe Sanh was part of a larger strategy when he and Johnson had determined "it was absolutely essential to hold the base."

Khe Sanh was the western anchor of the Marine forces, which had tactical responsibility of holding on to I Corps that included the five northernmost provinces of South Vietnam. Route 9 extended some eight to ten miles south of and parallel to the DMZ from Dong Ha over to the Khe Sanh base to the west (refer to maps A, B, and C, p. 23, 24, and 25). Khe Sanh was a major part of the Marines' defensive system, holding intact the DMZ while it was simultaneously being used as a blocking force. Route 9 then stretched to the Ho Chi Minh Trail area in the west, crossing into Laos.

The Ho Chi Minh Trail area was considered the supply line to all Communist forces in South Vietnam. The location of Khe Sanh was the reason the combat base was considered to be so important. Khe Sanh had its own airstrip, which supplied all the Marines who were fighting in the Ho Chi Minh Trail area while Route 9 was the main ground supply lifeline to the Marine base. The U.S. Marine combat base and its role of disrupting the flow of armament and supplies to the south made the base irreplaceable. In the eyes of President Johnson and General Westmoreland, the base was to be saved at all costs.

Yet it was sometimes said, when you were at Khe Sanh, you were nowhere. As the area was sparsely civilian populated and out in the middle of the wilderness, it presented the opportunity for the United States to use its devastating firepower.

The fall of 1967 was the perfect time and place to send Hanoi a message by using a tactical nuclear weapon on the gathering masses of enemy troops. At the same time, it would break a gaping hole into the Ho Chi Minh Trail. This would have sent the message. General Westmoreland also knew it would be a great psychological defeat for the enemy forces in the area and would put the fear of God in their surviving troops.

In 1959, Daniel Ellsberg was working for the RAND Corporation and, subsequently, the Defense Department. *After leaving RAND for the Defense Department in the Pentagon, he ultimately acquired close to a dozen special top secret clearances.* Daniel made clear to me there was zero chance of a Russian or Chinese nuclear response to such use of force by the United States in Vietnam.

It had been determined that only if a nuclear weapon was detonated on Russian or Chinese soil would there be a response in kind. A surgical strike with a tactical nuclear weapon in a sparsely civil populated area of the DMZ in Vietnam would not rise to such a level. It was my job to deploy the weapon and send the message to Hanoi.

During a visit to Daniel and his wife Patricia's home on June 15, 2019, with Angela at my side, Daniel told us of these facts. On this day Mr. Ellsberg also confirmed what he said in several of his books that John Paul Vann had been his closest friend in life. Then Mr. Ellsberg stated, *"Michael, you were the spearhead of the project."*

While Daniel was sitting and looking down at his kitchen table, he said, "In my opinion, I do believe what you strapped on that night was a *real atomic bomb*." His words sent a shiver through my spine. Daniel then looked up, put his hand on my shoulder, and said, "It's okay, Michael, heroes are allowed to cry too!"

Daniel Ellsberg and Michael.

Patricia and Daniel Ellsberg with
Michael and Angela Chapanar.

(Pictures courtesy of Michael Chapanar.)

The Doomsday Machine

Confessions of a Nuclear War Planner

DANIEL ELLSBERG

6-15-19

To Michael!

A true military hero
(they do occur, on both
sides of all wars, good
+ bad)

Who — thank God — was
allowed to carry out his
mission to the end!

BLOOMSBURY
NEW YORK · LONDON · OXFORD · NEW DELHI · SYDNEY

Semper Fidelis —

Dan Ellsberg

Mr. Ellsberg went on to ask me if I knew the United States had used nuclear weapons many times since the bombings of Nagasaki and Hiroshima in 1945. When I said I was not aware, he replied, "Most people are not aware." He explained, they had been used the precise way a gun was used when you pointed

365

it at someone's head in a direct confrontation, whether or not the trigger was pulled. For a certain type of gun owner, this might be the best use of the gun. It was why they had it, why they kept it loaded, and why it was at all times ready. All American presidents since Franklin Roosevelt had acted on that motive. The ability to threaten to initiate nuclear attacks if certain demands were not met were partial reasons for owning nuclear weapons. He went on to explain he listed in his book, *The Doomsday Machine: Confessions of a Nuclear War Planner*, the twenty-five most significant nuclear crises of the past one hundred years in chronological order. Daniel further stated he had listed the Khe Sanh ordeal in the number 14 slot. Angela and I were shocked as he grinned and reached for his book to show us page 320. Sure enough, the happening at Khe Sanh was listed. I read over the entire list of twenty-five when I noticed the word *correct* was used only one time. In the Khe Sanh listing, he utilized the word *correct*, and he even put it in parentheses. I then realized Dan's book was written in 2017, and the *New York Times* had not yet printed their article regarding Operation Fracture Jaw. The *Times* did not print the story regarding recently uncovered top secret documents until October 6, 2018. I asked Dan why he used the word *correct* when referring to nuclear weapons in the Khe Sanh situation. He replied, "Trust me, I was knowledgeable about your ordeal fifty years before the *New York Times* or *Washington Post.* I was a nuclear war planner." He then handed me his book to keep.

Prior to arriving at Daniel and Patricia's home, I was worried. I knew he only read a rough draft of my book, and I worried he might criticize or have doubts. When Angela and I arrived, with hesitation, I knocked on his door. Dan answered, stepped out onto the porch, hugged me, and said, "Michael, I loved your book." Then Patricia stepped to the door and reiterated, "We loved your book!" It was the vindication I had yearned for my entire life. Seconds later, this astute gentleman named Ellsberg looked at Angela and me and said, "I have only one question, whatever happened to Susie?"

* * *

In Vietnam Lieutenant General R. E. Cushman was General Hochmuth's superior officer. Two years after Hochmuth's death, Cushman became deputy director of the CIA from 1969 to 1971. Ellsberg, prior to turning himself in for trial, was in hiding along with his wife, Patricia. Meanwhile, CIA Deputy Director Cushman was on his trail, trying to apprehend him. According to Ellsberg, President Nixon was also just as worried about what additional material Dan copied, but not yet leaked and still had in his possession. The additional material thought to be copied was possible nuclear war planning during some of McNamara's days as secretary of defense, and that caught Nixon's attention.

Ellsberg actually did copy nuclear weapons information and plans. For this reason, Cushman was in hot pursuit. Daniel gave those papers to his brother Harry for safekeeping, and his brother kept them for two years. His brother then hid the papers in a trash dump. Harry ended up burying the papers in a cardboard box inside a garbage bag. He dug a hole on the side of a bluff above the dirt road that was bordering the dump and buried the bag. An old gas stove resting on the bluff identified the burial spot. Ironically and fortunately for the Ellsbergs, a near hurricane (tropical storm Doria) hit and washed the bag and its contents away, never to be found. Things do happen.

In close conversation with Mr. Ellsberg, I have come to believe even more what I have always thought to be true—that is, the night in Dong Ha at the airstrip when I boarded a helicopter with the bomb strapped on was not a drill!

In December 2006 Daniel Ellsberg was awarded the 2006 Right Livelihood Award in Stockholm, Sweden, for putting peace and truth first, at considerable personal risk, and dedicating his life to inspiring others to follow his example. He is also a senior fellow of the Nuclear Age Peace Foundation.

Shortly after our visit in June 2019 with Daniel and Patricia Ellsberg, Angela and I watched a movie *The Post*. The film is based on a true story, starring Meryl Streep and Tom Hanks. The movie details how the *Washington Post* staffers risked everything to publish the classified documents known as the Pentagon Papers that Ellsberg had leaked to the press. Coming to know Mr. Ellsberg, I believe, as he does, in placing peace and truth at the top of the list along with the urgent need for patriotic whistleblowing. Another movie worth watching is titled *"The Pentagon Papers"* starring James Spader.

On a personal note, I want to acknowledge and thank both Pat and Dan for playing a most important role in their effort to stop that terrible war.

* * *

Ellsberg meets Vann

Dan Ellsberg spoke very little to me about Major General Edward Lansdale. Lansdale retired as major general in the United States Air Force in 1963 and continued his work with the CIA. Ellsberg mentioned that Lansdale was involved in some bizarre cloak-and-dagger operations with the

Central Intelligence Agency over the years, and that's about all Dan would say.

After retirement, Lansdale went on to work for the secretary of defense in Washington DC and continued to be a senior officer in the CIA.

In 1965, President Johnson put Mr. Lansdale in charge of the pacification program in Vietnam. Ellsberg requested to be on his team and liked Lansdale for his commitment to democracy and their mutual thinking about the pacification program. Ellsberg then transferred from the Department of Defense to the State Department and was sent to Saigon on his team. Mr. Lansdale handed Ellsberg the assignment of going to many of the various provinces in South Vietnam and reporting back to him regarding the pacification efforts. At the time John Vann was working as an adviser to the U.S. Agency for International Development (AID) in South Vietnam. The first thing on Mr. Ellsberg's agenda was meeting Vann. Shortly after arriving in Saigon, Dan did meet up with John. Although both were technically civilians, they found themselves fighting side by side as comrades in the war. From there they became best of friends. How strange was it—John Vann, equivalent to a three-star general in the United States Army, was mysteriously killed in a helicopter crash without a shot being fired? He was killed the same week he was set to testify on Ellsberg's behalf. Our family will forever be suspicious of his mysterious death.

In 1989 Neil Sheehan wrote a Pulitzer Prize-winning book, *A Bright Shining Lie*. It is an eight-hundred-page detailed account of Vann, the family, and a straightforward analysis of John's ten-year commitment to the war. There is also a 1998 HBO movie *A Bright Shining Lie* in which the great actor Bill Paxton portrays the part of my cousin.

CHAPTER 40

Looking Back

The DMZ, known as the dead Marine zone, and the area on the south side of the DMZ were nicknamed Leatherneck Square. It consisted of Gio Linh to Dong Ha to Cam Lo to Con Thien, and it was my home away from home for twelve months (refer to map B, p. 24).

Throughout this entire area, I was a roadrunner, here and there from day to day and week to week. Until records were declassified, I had no idea of what named combat operations were involved. I never knew in real time what combat operations I had participated in. I also didn't know at the time how many Marines or enemies were KIA (killed in action) or wounded. I had no reason to know the statistics until receiving intel regarding these types of things in Okinawa. There were always rumors in Vietnam, but with no real credibility.

Being embedded with so many different units, companies, and platoons made it impossible to keep track. It did not matter who you were with or where you were; artillery, rockets, and mortars followed. If we went two or three days without enemy fire, we would hope the conflict was winding down. Then *boom*, *bang*, and it was raining steel again.

The entire time in Vietnam no one talked of a countrywide enemy Tet Offensive attack being planned. Quite the opposite, we were supposedly winning by attrition. There was seemingly no possibility the enemy could muster up enough offense to try and overtake the entire country. The egos of President Johnson, McNamara, and General Westmoreland were now, perhaps, the driving forces of the war. In no way did Johnson, McNamara, or Westmoreland ever believe these little Vietnamese people could pull off a con job of such magnitude on the United States. But these smart little Vietnamese people did just that. Precisely sixty days after I left Vietnam, the Khe Sanh Combat Base was fiercely attacked and under desperate siege for seventy-seven straight days. The main event, Tet, started nine days later. Enemy forces were attempting to overrun South Vietnam. January 30 and 31 of 1968 will forever be remembered in history as the Tet Offensive attacks. American public support for the war went straight downhill from there. It was the beginning of the end for the United States winning the war in Vietnam.

We may never know how close the United States came to using a nuclear weapon two months prior to the siege of Khe Sanh and the Tet Offensive. The two Communist surprise attacks were both imminent after months and years of planning to set them in motion with enemy divisions gathering in the fall of 1967.

I believe the United States was within minutes of using a nuclear bomb on one very eerie night. Approximately sixty days prior to these two attacks, they strapped something on me in a frantic way. Forty-five minutes later, that same something was taken off and away. I pray every day we never come that close again.

* * *

*A most important segment of the
Vietnam War played out as follows:*

Robert McNamara, secretary of defense, announced his pending resignation on November 29, 1967. His announcement came just one week after I left Vietnam and less than three weeks after that frantic and terrifying night I strapped on the bomb. Within a week after I left Vietnam, McNamara was said to be harboring grave doubts about the war although what he knew at the time may never be known. Yet it is hard for me to believe he did not know what took place approximately three weeks earlier with a tactical nuclear weapon. It is well-documented that President Johnson did not want another Dien Bien Phu. How could Johnson explain to the American people that he allowed a repeat of Dien Bien Phu and the massacre of six thousand American Marines at Khe Sanh to take place? For this reason, Johnson was adamant about saving the base *at all costs*.

Whether or not McNamara was on board with all this would never be known for sure. Although General Westmoreland was definitely proven to be totally onboard when, in February 1968, he actually approved the plan, code named *Fracture Jaw*, to officially move nukes into Vietnam. When this official operation became known to others, it was quickly shut down, and all plans, notes, and communications were put into an airtight vault with no disclosure of content under positive security.

The unanswered question remains: will the unofficial or informal part of the operation to use a nuke in the fall of 1967 ever be uncovered? Quite possibly not, in light of the very few who were knowingly involved. I always felt, on that night, training, tactics, procedures, and protocols were not being followed per the field manual. Seemingly confusing decisions to activate were being made on the fly under the strictest of confidentiality. But then again, I was just a lance corporal delivery boy with the bomb.

Whatever took place with me on that night would certainly not be the first time an American president attempted to protect himself from a catastrophic defeat. The major enemy attacks to come truly were eminent, and the writing on the wall regarding the history to follow these attacks was very real. The downfall of a U.S. president, a secretary of defense, and a commanding general of the Vietnam War and the dramatic end of our most indispensable strategic base we called Khe Sanh all happened within a few short months thereafter.

McNamara's last day as defense secretary was said to be unforgettable. In a meeting on his last day he reeled off statistics on how, up to this point, we already dropped more bombs on Vietnam than all of Europe during World War II. While teary eyed, he stated, *"It hasn't done a fucking thing!"*[18]

In a memoir McNamara wrote in 1995, he stated, his own behavior in shaping the war was "wrong, terribly wrong." McNamara also admitted that he helped President Johnson deceive the press and American public about the war.

On February 29, 1968, Robert McNamara left the government. He went back to corporate life, serving as head of the World Bank for the next thirteen years.

President Johnson then announced on March 31, 1968, exactly sixty-one days after the start of the Tet Offensive attacks, that he would not accept his party's nomination, nor would he run for reelection. He essentially gave up. He was later said to be in a state of

---

[18] Oliver Stone and Pete Kuznik, *The Concise Untold History of the United States,* New York, Gallery Books, 2014

depression. His presidency ended on January 20, 1969. He was also said to have grown longer hair while becoming somewhat of a recluse.

General William Westmoreland was relieved of his command in June of 1968 as head of U.S. Military forces in Vietnam. His war of attrition positively did not work. Westmoreland went on to serve as chief of staff of the U.S. Army from 1968 to 1972 until his retirement.

On July 5, 1968, the indispensable Marine combat base at Khe Sanh was closed.

* * *

While the tactical nuclear weapon operation might have been rogue and covert in 1967, in 1968 Westmoreland attempted to make it official with others in the hierarchy. Although if Westmoreland thought we were winning the war of attrition, stating, "The end is in view," why did he move to officially acknowledge and approve Operation *Fracture Jaw* in January and early February of '68?

I believe all three—LBJ, McNamara, and Westy—understood we needed to do something completely different to win.

John Paul Vann's assessment of the war in the summer of 1967 proved to be true. We were not winning!

CHAPTER 41

Cheers to the FBI and CIA

One summer day in the mid-80s, some fifteen years after being discharged from the Marine Corps, I was in a restaurant/bar in Canton, Ohio, known as Cheers. I was sitting at the bar, eating lunch with a lifelong friend. My so-called friend was criticizing the Vietnam War efforts and accusing the United States of accomplishing nothing in Vietnam. He started getting personal regarding my efforts. I didn't realize he was half in the bag when I made a giant blunder.

I told him I was trained to deploy a nuclear weapon in 1967 to thwart off a possible overrun attack of one of our bases on the DMZ. He replied, "Sure, sure, and if my grandmother had balls, she would be my grandfather!" We ended up debating the nuclear issue. He also implied, I might have the perception I was an American hero in the Vietnam conflict. I corrected his perception and informed him I was an ordinary guy who was given the opportunity to train for something extraordinary, no more and no less. There was no one else sitting at the bar that late afternoon. We were talking in a moderate, low tone. The female bartender was listening and joined in with her own thoughts on the war. It was my understanding she had a family member who was with the police department. Later that day the female bartender told her family member about the conversation, and the police chief told the FBI.

One week later in Cheers, I was having my usual Friday lunch. I was sitting at a table and had a view of the outside parking lot. I noticed an all-white, unmarked vehicle with several antennas and a government license plate pull up and park in front of the window. Two men in suits got out of the vehicle and entered the restaurant/bar. One of the men asked the bartender if Michael Chapanar was still in the bar. Like the New York Yankee catcher Yogi Berra once said, "It's déjà vu all over again." It was sounding to me like a similar situation that happened years ago in an Oceanside bar when three MPs walked in and asked the same question, "Is Michael Chapanar in the bar?" Exactly like before, the bartender's index finger pointed straight to me. Both men walked over with stern faces, and one of them showed an ID. Sure enough, he was with the FBI. They were polite, but stern, asking for my identification and verifying my name. I was invited to join them at a booth next to a window far away from the bar and other tables. They proceeded to talk to me about a conversation that took place seven days earlier in the bar, regarding Vietnam and a nuclear weapon. They asked if I knew anything about the conversation. I replied, "Yes." I knew there was no point in denying the brief and non-in-depth conversation I had with a friend.

They continued to be businesslike, but noticed my glass was empty. One of the gentlemen summoned the waitress, and she asked if I wanted a beer. I replied, "Why not?" I knew I was not going to get a beer behind bars.

I asked if I could buy them one; they declined and informed me they were still on the clock.

Surprisingly, they acknowledged my importance in Vietnam and thanked me for my service. They said they were here to let me know my records were still classified and asked me if I was aware of this. I let them know I thought they were probably still classified, and I made a blunder. I told them it was not a detailed conversation, and I would not talk about it again to anyone.

Both gentlemen put me at ease, stating they were not there to threaten me, just to let me know the records were still classified. They said it would be a good idea to keep a low profile on the entire incident and issue. I agreed, and they were satisfied. I was relieved I was not going to prison and concluded I was never going to make the same mistake again.

I surmised, the one gentleman who did not present his ID might be with the CIA. As they ended the conversation, he said, "Thank you for your service with the USMC and also the work you did in Okinawa and Vietnam with our agency." That told me all I needed to know. He was definitely with the CIA.

They finished up their remarks and said they had to get back up north. I assumed they were talking about going back up to Cleveland. The whole thing was embarrassing, but I had learned a lesson. I vowed never to make that blunder again.

CHAPTER 42

Dress Blues

The day I visited the Marine Corps Recruiter's Office, two Marine sergeant recruiters talked about "the few, the proud, the Marines." They were very cordial and distinguished in their dress blues. There were a lot of medals and ribbons pinned on with striking insignias and colorful patches of rank on each sleeve. The shooting medals hanging on their chest were most impressive. They had me watching slide presentations of career opportunities and handed out informative brochures. They said the corps offered a unique opportunity to travel the world with a steady paycheck.

Both recruiters stated, the Marine Corps would teach me a specialty job that I could pursue a career with in civilian life. It was a very exciting presentation. The music playing during the slideshow gave me goose bumps; it was uplifting and emotional. Some slides depicted the wonderful health care you would receive while in the corps and for the rest of your life. It was overwhelming to an eighteen-year-old teenager. It was an opportunity of a lifetime and one you could not pass up, knowing you were going to be drafted soon. I told the recruiters I was not thinking of staying in for more than two years. They said, "That's okay. When you are discharged in two years, you will have a great civilian career in front of you." I felt good knowing my future was secure. Serving only twenty-two months in the Marine Corps, I ended up an honorably discharged and mentally and physically ailing twenty-year-old. I was also at the bottom of the financial barrel. The daily payout for a lance corporal, including combat pay, was $6.03, or about $181.00 per month. Today my dress-green Marine Corps uniform hangs in the closet with only the rank of private first class sewn on the sleeves. I never had an opportunity while serving, or felt the need after discharge, to sew on the rank of lance corporal. The National Defense Ribbon is the only ribbon to ever hang on my uniform. I never did get to wear the dress-blue Marine Corps uniform I had dreamed of wearing— no chance, no time, and no money to buy the uniform.

Oddly enough, I was never ordered to qualify with a Marine Corps handgun, yet so many of the duties in Nam required carrying the .45-caliber semiautomatic pistol. I was prohibited from carrying a long gun or rifle while putting in or taking out mines and was only permitted to carry a holstered .45

with a bayonet for probing when minesweeping. Qualifying at the pistol range with a .45 was a USMC oversight. Bottom line, there was no shooting medal to hang on my uniform. I didn't even receive a rifle qualification acknowledgement until records were declassified and updated in 2012. I never fired a handgun until experiencing ground action in Vietnam, and I don't know if I ever hit anything with it. God only knows. Using a rifle or a long gun was a different story.

Now discharged, it was time to somehow pick up life and act like a normal twenty-year-old. The reception from a lot of other young people was not good. Even though I was a social young man, in many ways I had become an unwelcomed citizen of the United States of America.

Just happy to be home, I was learning to accept it. I respected the opinion of others about the war. In many ways I agreed with those who were against the Vietnam War. Yet if called upon today, I would consider it a privilege and an honor to serve again.

I love this country and all the people in it. You have an opportunity to live free and be in charge of your own destiny. Everyone can agree to disagree. America allows each and every one to have their own belief system. For these reasons I would again stand up for the country and will forever be a United States Marine.

The United States of America is the greatest force on the planet for peace, justice, and freedom in history.

CHAPTER 43

Health Issues

After being discharged from active duty, I had several health issues I needed to address with the Veterans Administration: ears ringing (tinnitus) and hypersensitive hearing (hyperacusis), also collapsed flatfeet and terrible memories of war—issues I still deal with today.

I had an appointment with the VA claims manager in Canton, Ohio, and was completely surprised to learn we attended high school together. We occasionally even hung around together back then. He said to bring the original DD-214 and Record of Service form with me for the appointment.

While looking over my Record of Service document, he was asking a lot of questions. When the answers did not match the Record of Service form, he had doubts and said I was being disingenuous with him. On the Record of Service form, the Marine Corps omitted all nuclear weapons training and my primary MOS 1372.

The DD-214 separation record was considered the bible of all documents a military person received upon discharge. If the DD-214 form was the bible, the USMC sure did change the scriptures. My DD-214 form made no sense at all. The Marine Corps stated I was a construction carpenter in the corps. It also stated I was equivalent to a construction foreman in civilian life.

I was never trained to use a hammer or a saw in the Marine Corps, let alone be labeled a civilian carpenter construction foreman. I'm sure the Marine Corps did what they had to do for national security reasons, knowing America was bigger than any one person. The VA representative concluded, my Record of Service form and my DD-214 form both spoke for themselves, and they had no further time for nonsense. My issues were denied. I concluded I had no further time for the Veterans Administration. Angela and I had bills to pay. At the time, the VA acted as if I were disingenuous at best. If the VA did not want to help, then what could I do? I realized, until the records were declassified, the Veterans Administration would not have the facts and true records to work with and review.

The VA was dealing with World War I vets, World War II vets, and Korean War vets. The VA was now being inundated and over-whelmed with Vietnam vets.

When visiting the Canton, Ohio, VA facility, there were never any seats left to sit or room to stand inside the building. They did not have the time, facilities, or manpower in the '60s and '70s to deal with the influx of Vietnam veterans.

Forty years later, I'm living with claustrophobia, PTSD, ear ringing, hypersensitive hearing, and collapsed flatfeet. I have endured many surgical operations on my feet alone. Because I was bounced around a lot in war, both jaw joints had to be replaced with titanium temporal mandibular joint replacements. I also had a cervical neck fusion, installing a steel H-plate and six screws along with a lower lumbar fusion with a rod, screws, and bone grafts. The VA did not provide for any of the operations. One good thing could be said: the taxpayer was never burdened with the cost of my surgeries. If not in the military, I would have never experienced injuries to this degree. Having to carry heavy weight, jumping out of aircraft, and also squatting four hundred eighty pounds took their toll. Incoming heavy artillery, rockets, mortars, Agent Orange, and seeing U.S. Marines and other human beings destroyed did the rest. I made so many adjustments in life that, literally, no one was aware of these issues. I learned to deal with constant pain while living a so-called normal life. I've undergone many serious surgical operations to stay active. I even had open-heart bypass surgery twelve years ago to fix a congenital heart defect. I was born with a pea-sized hole in the heart that never closed after birth, and I have no idea how I was accepted into the Marine Corps. Heart surgeons performed by-pass surgery and sewed in a Teflon umbrella to close the hole, and there were no further problems with the heart. Prostate cancer was brought on from being exposed to a chemical called Agent Orange, and fifteen years ago the prostate was surgically removed. Once again, no money was paid out by the

Veterans Administration, and the VA never performed any of these operations.

In 2004 the hypersensitive hearing and tinnitus (ringing of the ears) were so overwhelming, I couldn't cope with them anymore. When visiting the Cleveland clinic, the only thing they could do was try injections of cortisone through my eardrums into the cochlea, which they did. They also prescribed 6 mg of Xanax per day for over a year, but the hearing problems were still overwhelming. The clinic recommended I go to the Baltimore hyperacusis and tinnitus clinic. Upon the second trip to Baltimore, I was fitted with hearing instruments in an attempt to tone down the hypersensitivity by retraining the brain. I was also told the ringing would probably never go away. They said if I wore the instruments in my ears for eighteen months to three years, it could help retrain the brain and lower the hypersensitivity to outside sounds. I had to try. It was like wearing buzzers in your ears, and it took months of wearing them longer and longer each day to acclimate to the buzzing. The instruments and trips to Baltimore cost thousands of dollars; the VA did not pay for any of the cost. Dr. Jasterboff at the Baltimore clinic said the brain would not retrain unless I weaned off Xanax. Coming off Xanax was not easy. After two years the hypersensitive hearing was slightly calming down, and I could finally turn up the television to a somewhat normal volume, but the ringing was as bad as ever.

In 2009 I visited UC Irvine Medical Center in California and was fitted with a new type of instrument therapy. I wore them for two years, but they were unsuccessful. It was now the promised land, or live with the condition. I decided I couldn't leave Angela just yet.

When my records were declassified, the Veterans Administration started to take me seriously. In 2013 the VA finally wanted to help although my primary-care physician said he didn't believe the severity of my hearing problems were as bad as I made out. He didn't understand why I constantly inserted silicone in both ears to reduce normal outside noises. He didn't even care to look at my past hearing hyperacusis medical history records. He said he didn't have time and referred me to a VA hearing specialist. After going through quite a process, the VA finally prescribed and provided a pair of hearing instruments. I couldn't tolerate the noise they made, but the VA did try. Intently listening to the faint sounds of a mine detector while at the same time absorbing the ear-piercing sound of explosions turned the hearing volume up and changed my life forever.

In the last year things have vastly improved, and I have a new VA primary-care doctor, Dr. Tran. On June 6, 2019, I had my first appointment with the new doctor. I was seated in Dr. Tran's office and waiting for the doctor to finish looking over past records. Finally, she walked in and started asking questions. The doctor asked if I had always taken vitamins. I said, "Yes." She asked where I purchased them; I replied, "Usually, the Target store."

The doctor shook her head and said, "Starting now, the VA will provide you with your vitamins, and you don't have to pay for them anymore." Dr. Tran then asked me to stand up as she wanted to give me a hug for serving in Vietnam. It was like a miracle; she hugged me and said, "Thank you for your service." It is good to have Dr. Tanya Tran as my primary-care physician. She is cordial and treats her patients with dignity. Things have come full circle. *Dr. Tanya Tran, of all things, is Vietnamese!*

Dr. Tanya Tran and Michael.

(Picture courtesy of Michael Chapanar.)

CHAPTER 44

Airtight Secrets

When in Vietnam, waiting for the flight back to the United States, a Marine officer handed me a two-inch-thick sealed packet of documents to carry back. I did not realize what I had in my possession at the time.

After landing at Marine Corps Air Station El Toro in California, I had no choice, but to go over the hill for two days and somehow return undetected with less than fifty-nine days to serve.

While over the hill and staying with Uncle John for the two days, I surgically cut open the packet and found some of my records and orders. I copied about half the documents (like an Ellsberg) and kept them under lock and key at home for over forty-five years. Fifty-one years later the government has given me permission to tell the story. In addition, I received the following records after being discharged.

The Record of Service form covers the date I entered service, from January 26, 1966, to the date of discharge, December 7, 1967. This official record has no entry to indicate the Military Occupation Specialty (MOS) 1372. All MOS 1372 assignments, dates, and places are completely omitted. Because of these omissions, the VA thought I was being disingenuous with them from the start.

There is no listing of nuclear weapon
designations or activities on this form.

Record of Service Form

RECORD OF SERVICE

ORGANIZATION	DATE	REASON	PRIMARY DUTY	GENERAL MILITARY (SUBJECTS)	DUTY	CONDUCT	SIGNATURE OF MARKING OFFICER
1st RTBN RTR MCRD SDIEGO	26 JAN 1966	JD	9900 RECRUIT				Bennett By dir 32 66 34102
1st RTBN RTR MCRD SDIEGO	1 APR 1966	Tr	9900 RECRUIT	4.3	4.2	4.0	Bennett By dir 42 66 34102
S co. MCRD RTR	APR 2	Tr	Joins RT				18-66 93288
S	APR 21 1966		Joins Tr		4.4	4.4	Bruce K. Davis CO
SU #1, 1stScolCo MCES, MCB, CAMLEJ, N. C.	MAY 17 1966	Jd	1371 DUINS				OIC
SU-#1, 1stScolCo MCES, MCB, CAMLEJ, N. C.	JUN 24 1966	Tr	1371 DUINS		4.5	4.1	By dir
CO"A"8thENGRBN FORTRS,FMFLant,CLNC	25Jun1966	Jd	CbtEngr 1371				ByDir 104-66/21313
CO"A"8thENGRBN FORTRS,FMFLant,CLNC	1 JUL 1966	Semi-Ann	CbtEngr 1371	4.0	4.3	4.3	Traverse CO
CO"A"8thENGRBN FORTRS,FMFLant,CLNC	1Aug66	Tr	CbtEngr 1371				Franqui CO 147-66/21313
"A"Co11thEngrBn5th MarDivCamPenCalif	28Sp66	Jd	CbtEngr 1371				Webster CO 04-66/21383
10Oct66 Redesig to "A" Co 11thEngrBn ForTrs FMFPA C CamPen 92055; 110ct66 Redesig fr "A" Co 11th EngrBn 5thMarDiv (-)(Rein) FMF CamPen 92055 auth Gr FMF msg 1105214							
	01NOV66	REDESIG TO A CO 11TH ENGRBN FMFPAC MCO 159 AUTH FORTRP FMFPAC HQO 011915Z NOV66					
"A"Co 11thEngrBn FMFPAC FFO SPRAN 9660c	31Jan67	Semi/Ann	1371 Cbt Engr	4.0	4.1	3.9	acting Bs
"A"Co 11th EngrBn FMFPAC FFO SPRAN	31Jul67	Semi-Ann	1371 CbtEngr		4.3	4.4	C. Pope CO UDM197-67/21383
"A"Co 11thEngrBn FMFPAC FFO SPRAN SEP SEC MCRS EL TORO	22Nov67	Tr	Cbt Engr		4.6	4.7	R.L. Reagan CO
SANTA ANA, CALIFORNIA SEP SEC MCAS EL TORO SANTA ANA, CALIFORNIA	22Nov67	Jd	AntgRelAcDu				ByDir Sgt
ACROSC MCRF (CRTR)Mo.	01Dec67	RelAcDu Jd	None				Sgt
RMC, Mo.	8Dec67		Inactive				Sgt
	220104	DISCH	Inactive				Sgt

EMBOSSED PLATE IMPRESSION

CHAPAMAR, MICHAEL P.   M

NAME (Last)	(First)	(Middle)	SERVICE NO.

NAVMC 118(3)-PD (Rev. 6-62) SUPERSEDES PREVIOUS EDITION WHICH WILL BE USED

C30780

* * *

Combat history—Expeditions— Awards record

The first entry on this record, dated January 8, 1967, reads, "Participated in counterinsurgency operations against the Communist (Viet Cong) forces in the Republic of Vietnam from December 3, 1966, to November 22, 1967." This record acknowledges my participation in ten combat operations although the Awards section is a mystery. The Awards section of the record indicates only three awards. The first two awards I earned before going to Vietnam were the National Defense Service Medal, dated May 5, 1966, and the Vietnam Service Medal, dated December 3, 1966. After serving six months in Vietnam, the Vietnam Campaign Medal was awarded on June 3, 1967. These three awards were basic medals earned by all military personnel who served in support of operations in the Republic of Vietnam during the Vietnam era. The Awards section does not list the Shooting Rifle Marksman Badge/Medal I earned at Camp Pendleton before going to Vietnam. The USMC did not acknowledge I used a weapon of any kind, and there is no mention of a Combat Action Ribbon. Until 2012 I was without any additional awards.

In conclusion, after living nearly fifty years with few medals, no tattoos, and no dress blues, I was not in search of glory. All I ever wanted to do was serve my country, standing up for freedom in America, and I was very fortunate to have done so.

Combat History-Expeditions-Awards Record

I was not aware of the combat operations record until 2012 at which time I also received an updated and partially corrected DD-215 form.

COMBAT HISTORY—EXPEDITIONS—AWARDS RECORD

COMBAT HISTORY—EXPEDITIONS

DATE OF ENTRY	DETAILS	FROM (DAY)	TO —	SIGNATURE
JAN 8 1967	PARTICIPATED IN COUNTER-INSURGENCY OPERATIONS AGAINST THE COMMUNIST (VIET CONG) FORCES IN THE REPUBLIC OF VIET NAM.		22Nov67 DEC 03 1986	*R. Garcia* Bydir
21Mar67	Participated in Operation Prairie I	3Dec66	7Mar67	
21Mar67	Participated in Operation Prairie II	8Mar67	17Mar67	*Louis C. Ray* CO
21Mar67	Participated in Operation Prairie III	18Mar67	19Apr67	*Louis C. Ray* CO
5Apr67	Participated in Operation Prairie IV	20Apr67	16May67	*L.E. Barge* Bydir
2Jun67	Participated in Operation Hickory	17May67	31May67	*L.E. Barge* Bydir
5Jun67	Participated in Operation Cimarron	1Jun67	2Jul67	*L.E. Barge* Bydir
8Jul67	Participated in Operation Buffalo	2Jul67	14Jul67	*L.E. Barge* Bydir
20Jul67	Participated in Operation Hickory II	14Jul67	16Jul67	*Louis C. Ray* CO
20Jul67	Participated in Operation King Fisher	16Jul67	19Jul67		Bydir
30Jul67	Participated in Operation Lancaster	18Jul67		*J.J. Wm* Bydir
20Jul67	Participated in Operation Kingfisher	16Jul67	1Nov67		Bydir
1Nov67	Participated in Operation Kentucky	1Nov67	22Nov67	*J.J. Jeannetti* Bydir

AWARDS

DESCRIPTION	STARS, DEVICES	DATE APPROVED	APPROVED BY	DATE MEDAL ISSUED	SIGNATURE
NDSM		3Jan66	SecNav		*W.D. Raschel...*
VSM	*/*.	3Dec66	SecNavInstr 1650.?		*William...* CO
VSM	w/*.	3Dec66	CO, 11thEngrBn RO 11231		*R. Garcia* Bydir
VSM w/Device(1960-		3Jun67	CO, 11thEngr Bn		*L.E. Barge* Bydir

EMBOSSED PLATE IMPRESSION

CHAPMAN, MICHAEL P.   E 3203XXX

| NAME (Last) | (First) | (Middle) | SERVICE NO. |

HAVMC 118(9)-PD (REV. 7-63) SUPERSEDES 11—23 EDITION WHICH WILL BE USED.

U.S. GOVERNMENT PRINTING OFFICE : 1963 OF—673584

Updated and corrected DD-215 form.

On January 3, 2012, the Marine Corps issued a partial correction to the old DD-214 form. The more corrected version added the following:

> VIETNAM SERVICE
> MEDAL (w/2 bronze stars)
>
> COMBAT ACTION
> RIBBON
>
> PRESIDENTIAL UNIT
> CITATION RIBBON
>
> RIFLE MARKSMAN
> BADGE
>
> REPUBLIC
> OF VIETNAM
> MERITORIOUS UNIT
> CITATION (Gallantry
> Cross Color w/Palm)

REPUBLIC
OF VIETNAM
MERITORIOUS UNIT
CITATION (Civil Actions,
First Class Color w/Palm)

CAUTION: NOT TO BE USED FOR IDENTIFICATION PURPOSES   ANY ALTERATIONS IN SHADED AREAS RENDER FORM VOID

CORRECTION TO DD FORM 214,
CERTIFICATE OF RELEASE OR DISCHARGE FROM ACTIVE DUTY

1. NAME (Last, First, Middle) CHAPANAR, MICHAEL PAUL	2. DEPT, COMPONENT AND BRANCH USMCR (J)	3. SOCIAL SECURITY NUMBER (Also, Service Number if applicable)		
4. MAILING ADDRESS (Include ZIP Code) 2430 PRESSER RD., AKRON, OH 44312				

5. ORIGINAL DD FORM 214 IS CORRECTED AS INDICATED BELOW:

ITEM NO.	CORRECTED TO READ
	SEPARATION DATE ON DD FORM 214 BEING CORRECTED: 7 DEC 67
24.	64369-2012-9331-TW DELETE: VIETNAM SERVICE MEDAL w/1* ADD: VIETNAM SERVICE MEDAL (w/2 bronze stars) COMBAT ACTION RIBBON PRESIDENTIAL UNIT CITATION RIBBON RIFLE MARKSMAN BADGE REPUBLIC OF VIETNAM MERITORIOUS UNIT CITATION (Gallantry Cross Color w/Palm) REPUBLIC OF VIETNAM MERITORIOUS UNIT CITATION (Civil Actions, First Class Color w/Palm) **

6. DATE (YYYYMMDD)	7. OFFICIAL AUTHORIZED TO SIGN			
	a. TYPED NAME (Last, First, Middle Initial)	b. GRADE	c. TITLE	d. SIGNATURE
20120103 MMSB/TW	STANZE, M. D.	CWO3	MCLNO, NPRC	

DD FORM 215, FEB 2000   PREVIOUS EDITION IS OBSOLETE.   MEMBER - 1
FormFlow/Adobe Professional 7.0

* * *

Unintended consequences
of a secret mission

The Record of Service form and separate
old DD-214 form both clearly depict how

secret the ADM missions were. I lived with these secrets for forty-five years.

The Record of Service form normally lists a Marine's primary Military Occupation Specialty (MOS) and, if applicable, any secondary MOS designation throughout his/her military career. It is also a permanent record of times, places, and dates of all training and proficiency. The Record of Service form is supposedly a record of who you were, what you did, and how well you performed.

There are fifteen separate signatures on my Record of Service form that attest to some of what I did, but certainly not all.

There is *no* entry of my primary MOS 1372, atomic demolitions munition. Consequently, this record prevented the securing of several skillful, high-paying jobs in civilian life. In 1968 a perspective mining employer/owner interviewed me and wanted to hire an explosives expert for his mining business. He took a look at my records and stated he couldn't find any reason to hire me based on the skills and training listed. Although the DD-214 listed a specialty number and title of 1372 ADM tech, the form went on to explain a related civilian occupation as "carpenter, construction foreman." Had I applied for a carpenter/foreman's job in civilian life, I would have been fired the first day. I was not a carpenter, let alone a foreman. Early after being discharged from active duty, I found these two significant documents were not going to be much help in the future. The Record of Service and DD-214 were permanent records I could not correct.

Both records are very important when applying for veteran's benefits. Upon explaining to the VA rep what my duties consisted of in the service, the representative read over the records and said I was being disingenuous. In essence, the records were handing the

Veterans Administration various reasons to deny claims, and I was now facing a real-life conundrum.

Not until the records were updated and somewhat corrected did the facts start to surface. I do not understand all the reasons it had to be done this way, but upon correction, a heavy burden was lifted. Quite possibly now, I can square myself with the world.

Why did the Marine Corps write up the official records in this manner? It certainly was a way of denying all classified nuclear weapon activity assigned to me and keeping *airtight secrets.*

CHAPTER 45

Permission Requested

On March 7, 2018, I mailed letters to President Trump, Secretary of Defense James Mattis, and Marine Corps Commandant General Robert B. Neller, requesting authorization from each to disclose the untold story.

The letters were sent via U.S. Postal Service certified mail.

* * *

Transcript of the letter I sent to the president, the secretary of defense, and the commandant of the Marine Corps

Dear President Trump:
March 7, 2018

I was born on April 26, 1947. I volunteered and joined the Marine Corps in January, 1966. Later that year I volunteered for Vietnam. At this point, I was a 1371 (Combat Engineer). I was then given the opportunity to volunteer for an ADM Team (Atomic Demolition Munition MOS 1372). I served a 12-month tour of duty from November 1966 to December 1967 in Vietnam. Prior to going to Vietnam, I was sent to San Diego Naval Air Station for ADM training.

While serving my entire tour on the DMZ in Vietnam, I was called out of the field 3 different times (each time for 10 days) to go to Okinawa for continuous training and updated Intel on enemy troops and our own escape routes. We all knew the mission would be a one-way-street.

There was approximately 3 Divisions of NVA gathering in the north-western section of South Vietnam on the DMZ. My mission when called upon was to jump in and either delay or destroy a massive ground force attack on one of our forward bases such as Khe Sanh or Con Thien.

In the fall of 1967, I was working in Leatherneck Square on the DMZ putting in and taking out mines; also, mine sweeping various sections of Route 9 to Khe Sanh. At the time the monsoons were starting and the season would be full blown through January. This obviously would limit our B52's and overall air strike support during these times. Therefore, one of the options General Westmoreland had in the playbook was the possibility of using a tactical nuclear weapon on the masses that could overrun one or more of our most forward fire bases. My mission was to save 4,000–6,000 Marines from being slaughtered.

The National Archives Center for Vietnam at Texas Tech University knows very little if much at all about the above. Ken Burns and Lynn Novik did a 10-part series called "The Vietnam War" which first aired in the fall of 2017. They did not reference any of the above.

My team and mission to save a base such as Con Thien from an overrun slaughter was highly classified. It is my understanding that in 2012 my records were declassified. At that time I was sent a new DD214 form updated DD215.

Many people if not everyone wants to hear my history. People refer to my ADM team as a "Green Light" team today. They also refer to the Atomic Weapon (Tactical Nuclear Weapon) I carried as a "Back-pack Nuclear Weapon" today.

With the utmost praise and loyalty for our country, I do not want to inadvertently do anything wrong. The National Archives, as well as a few movie directors are interested in my story. I would like to have your opinion. Would I be harming the country by telling my story to the world? I have all my original orders and medical records from the time I served in the USMC. As stated, these are all originals and there can be no doubt about the facts of this story.

What would you do if you were me?

I have been married and will celebrate my 50th Wedding Anniversary on May 4, 2018. I believe by telling this story it will alter our lives somewhat going forward (including monetarily.)

Although I have been a guest speaker at local veteran clubs, a high school and on a US Navy War Ship here in San Diego all within the past couple of years, I have only skimmed and told the highlights of the story to these various organizations.

I have all the nuts and bolts of my training and activities in combat of which, as of yet, I have not entirely disclosed.

Although I believe the American people and our Armed Forces would benefit from knowing this history, there is a little voice inside of me that says I may be doing something that could be detrimental or harmful to the USA.

Please advise ASAP. Please feel free to call me (h)

xxx-xxx-xxxx or (cell) xxx-xxx-xxxx or you can email me at xxxxxx@xxx.com.

Sincerely,
Michael P. Chapanar
Registered Mail of this
letter has also been sent to:
General Robert B.
Neller, Commandant
of the USMC
General Mattis,
Secretary of Defense

* * *

Responses and answers

In reply to these letters, I received a very personal appreciation letter from President Donald J. Trump, dated June 15, 2018. I also received a separate letter on behalf of the secretary of defense and the United States Marine Corps in April 2018.

Transcription of letter received on behalf of the secretary of defense and the United States Marine Corps, dated April 24, 2018, is as follows:

Dear Mr. Chapanar,

Thank you for your letter of March 7, 2018. I am responding on behalf of the Secretary of Defense. Although my office has conducted an extensive search, we have been unable to discover few details _beyond_ what you have offered in your letter. *Foreign Policy magazine* of 30 January 2014 had an article that covered the basics of the program much as you did in your letter. The *Rusi*

Journal, in April 2008, published a very similar article. *The Marine Corps University Library has a training manual that discusses the tactical nuclear weapon. It is our opinion* that should you choose to tell your story of the training and potential use of the tactical nuclear weapon, that *you will not cause any harm nor will it be in any way detrimental to the United States of America or the Marine Corps.*"

Again, thank you for your letter.

Sincerely,
Paul J. Weber
Acting Director
Marine Corps History

UNITED STATES MARINE CORPS
MARINE CORPS UNIVERSITY
EDUCATION COMMAND
HISTORY DIVISION
2044 BROADWAY
QUANTICO, VIRGINIA 22134-5067

April 24, 2018

Mr. Michael P. Chapanar
~~████████████████████~~
~~████████████████████~~

Dear Mr. Chapanar,

Thank you for your letter of March 7, 2018. I am responding on behalf the Secretary of Defense. Although my office has conducted an extensive search, we have been able to discover few details beyond what you have offered in your letter. *Foreign Policy* magazine of 30 January 2014 had an article that covered the basics of the program much as you did in your letter. The *RUSI Journal,* in April 2008, published a very similar article. The Marine Corps University Library has a training manual that discusses the tactical nuclear weapon.

It is our opinion that should you choose to tell your story of the training and potential use of the tactical nuclear weapon, that you will not cause any harm nor will it be in any way detrimental to the United States of America or the Marine Corps.

Again, thank you for your letter.

Sincerely,

Raul J. Weber
Acting Director,
Marine Corps History

Department of Defense Reply Letter

After receiving permission, I wrote the book and submitted it to the Department of Defense for approval. On September 11, 2018, it was "cleared for open publication by the Department of Defense Office of Prepublication and Security Review."

Inexplicably, as with other coincidental and significant dates in my life, the book was approved for publication on September 11, 2018. It is a date the world has never forgotten (9/11).

Department of the Army Field Manual
Marine Corps Fleet Marine Force Manual

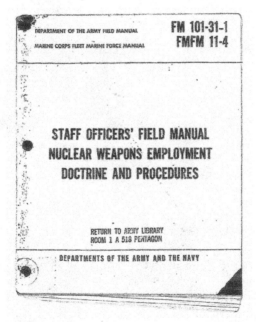

CHAPTER 46

Unexpected Meeting

In January 2020, a close friend Clifton D. Shuman and I were having lunch in the Skybox Grill and Tavern. The owner of the establishment, Mr. Donald A. Phinney, walked over to our table and cordially greeted us for lunch. Don noticed I was wearing a hat with a Marine Corps logo on it. He asked if I was a former Marine. I said yes and also let him know my friend Cliff was a retired colonel in the United States Air Force. It kicked off a good conversation. Cliff was a combat rescue Black Hawk helicopter pilot, and Don found him interesting. Don was asking Cliff details of his career, and in return Don shared with us his own twenty-year career highlights while serving in the United States Army. The conversation between these two American patriots was fascinating.

Colonel Shuman served his country in uniform for over thirty-two years, entering the military in 1978. In 1990 he was transferred to the Air Force Reserve, joining the Seventy-First Special Operations Squadron until it was reassigned as the Three Hundred Fifth Rescue Squadron in 1994. He has served in a variety of positions within the squadron, including instructor/flight examiner, chief of safety, flight commander, and assistant to the commander. Prior to promotion to colonel (O-6), he served as the commander of the Three Hundred Fifth Rescue Squadron, Davis-Monthan AFB, AZ. In the summer of 2005, Cliff commanded the 335th Expeditionary Rescue Squadron along with twenty-five reservists from the 920th Rescue

Wing. Under Cliff's command in "Operation Redwing," the team participated in the rescue of Marcus Luttrell. The lone survivor Navy SEAL, Luttrell, was on the run from the Taliban after all the other members of his SEAL team had been killed in an ambush during a covert operation.

In the bestselling novel, *Lone Survivor*, Luttrell documented his ordeal. Mark Wahlberg portrayed the part of Marcus Luttrell in the Hollywood movie also titled *Lone Survivor*. Colonel Shuman also had the honor and privilege to serve as the deputy director for contingency operations and plans under the White House Military Office (WHMO). His last assignment before retirement was as the deputy director for the Pentagon Office of Emergency Management.

Cliff is a command pilot with more than three thousand two hundred military hours in five different aircrafts and has deployed in support of Operation Desert Shield/Storm, Operation Provide Comfort II, Operation Northern Watch, Operation Southern Watch, and Operation Enduring Freedom. He recently retired from American Airlines where he served over twenty years as a 320 Airbus pilot. Colonel Shuman and I are also partners; we share interest in two airplanes.

Donald A. Phinney, master sergeant MOS 12B50/12E30, was on active duty from 1977 until retiring in 1997. He served six years as an atomic demolitions munitions (ADM) team chief. He was also a platoon sergeant in charge of four ADM teams while in Germany during the Cold War. Don was a true professional working with nuclear weapons. For fourteen of his twenty years, he served as a combat engineer.

Cliff was totally amazed when Don told us what he did in the Army. Cliff turned to me and said, "You and Michael have a lot in common." Don asked, "What does this former Marine and I have in common?" I enthusiastically jumped in and told him I was also a combat engineer and trained in atomic demolitions munitions. Don was surprised and began asking questions. At that point, Don was still cordial, but I could tell from his questioning, he thought I was suspect at best. The next day I returned for lunch, and he was not so cordial with his questions. Later that week Angela and I went to his restaurant for dinner, and Don was downright rude. He said he was in the process of investigating me. My wife was stunned. Don told both Angela and me that he was a man badly in need of some additional information and proof. He actually said to Angela that it would be very embarrassing if he finished his investigation and found me to be a joke.

Toward the end of January, I felt it necessary to let Don review my military records.

I let him examine all one hundred seventy-six personal records, documents, and original orders signed by my commanders and Marine Corps generals. After he carefully studied my records and upon completion of his own in-depth investigation, we became great friends. Because of this revelation, I asked Don if he would consider being a nuclear weapon technical adviser regarding any furtherance of my story. To my astonishment, he accepted and said he would be honored and proud to help me with anything I needed. Cliff Shuman and Don Phinney are great American patriots. Go, Air Force, and go, Army! All three of us bleed red, white, and blue, and those are wonderful colors.

The End

INDEX

A

B

C

J

K

L

O

P

T

V

W

ABOUT THE AUTHOR

Michael Chapanar is retired and living in sunny Southern California with his wife, Angela. Michael is enjoying life watching baseball, playing golf, skydiving, and flying airplanes.

CPSIA information can be obtained
at www.ICGtesting.com
Printed in the USA
BVHW061039240321
603332BV00001B/57